Eternal Sabbath

VOL. 7

Fuyumi Soryo

Translated and adapted by
Ikoi Hiroe

Lettered by
H. Jones

DEL REY

Ballantine Books • New York

A Del Rey Trade Paperback Original

Published in the United States by Del Rey Books, an imprint of The Random House Publishing Group, a division of Random House, Inc., New York.

Del Rey is a registered trademark and the Del Rey colophon is a trademark of Random House, Inc.

Publication rights arranged through Kodansha Ltd.

First published in Japan in 2004 by Kodansha Ltd., Tokyo.

ISBN 978-0-345-49194-7

Printed in the United States of America

www.delreymanga.com

9 8 7 6 5 4 3 2 1

Translator/adapter: Ikoi Hiroe
Lettering: H. Jones

Contents

Honorifics Explained

Throughout the Del Rey Manga books, you will find Japanese honorifics left intact in the translations. For those not familiar with how the Japanese use honorifics and, more important, how they differ from American honorifics, we present this brief overview.

Politeness has always been a critical facet of Japanese culture. Ever since the feudal era, when Japan was a highly stratified society, use of honorifics —which can be defined as polite speech that indicates relationship or status—has played an essential role in the Japanese language. When addressing someone in Japanese, an honorific usually takes the form of a suffix attached to one's name (example: "Asuna-san"), is used as a title at the end of one's name, or appears in place of the name itself (example: "Negi-sensei," or simply "Sensei!").

Honorifics can be expressions of respect or endearment. In the context of manga and anime, honorifics give insight into the nature of the relationship between characters. Many English translations leave out these important honorifics and therefore distort the feel of the original Japanese. Because Japanese honorifics contain nuances that English honorifics lack, it is our policy at Del Rey not to translate them. Here, instead, is a guide to some of the honorifics you may encounter in Del Rey Manga.

-san: This is the most common honorific and is equivalent to Mr., Miss, Ms., or Mrs. It is the all-purpose honorific and can be used in any situation where politeness is required.

-sama: This is one level higher than "-san." It is used to confer great respect.

-dono: This comes from the word "tono," which means "lord." It is an even higher level than "-sama" and confers utmost respect.

-kun: This suffix is used at the end of boys' names to express familiarity or endearment. It is also sometimes used by men among friends, or when addressing someone younger or of a lower station.

-chan: This is used to express endearment, mostly toward girls. It is also used for little boys, pets, and even among lovers. It gives a sense of childish cuteness.

Bozu: This is an informal way to refer to a boy, similar to the English terms "kid" and "squirt."

Sempai/ Senpai: This title suggests that the addressee is one's senior in a group or organization. It is most often used in a school setting, where underclassmen refer to their upperclassmen as "sempai." It can also be used in the workplace, such as when a newer employee addresses an employee who has seniority in the company.

Kohai: This is the opposite of "sempai" and is used toward underclassmen in school or newcomers in the workplace. It connotes that the addressee is of a lower station.

Sensei: Literally meaning "one who has come before," this title is used for teachers, doctors, or masters of any profession or art.

[blank]: This is usually forgotten in these lists, but it is perhaps the most significant difference between Japanese and English. The lack of honorific means that the speaker has permission to address the person in a very intimate way. Usually, only family, spouses, or very close friends have this kind of permission. Known as *yobisute,* it can be gratifying when someone who has earned the intimacy starts to call one by one's name without an honorific. But when that intimacy hasn't been earned, it can be very insulting.

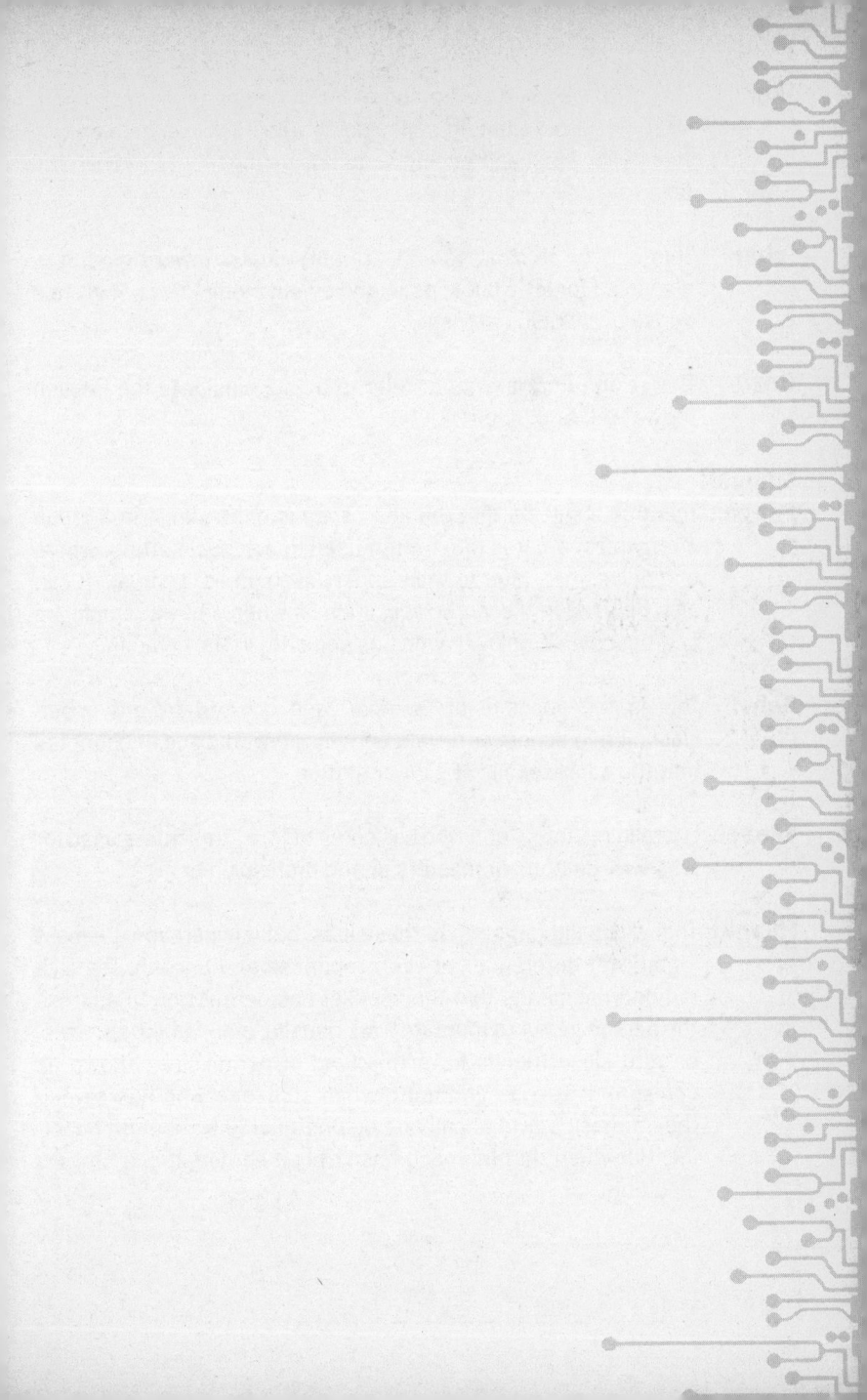

#61 DISCORD

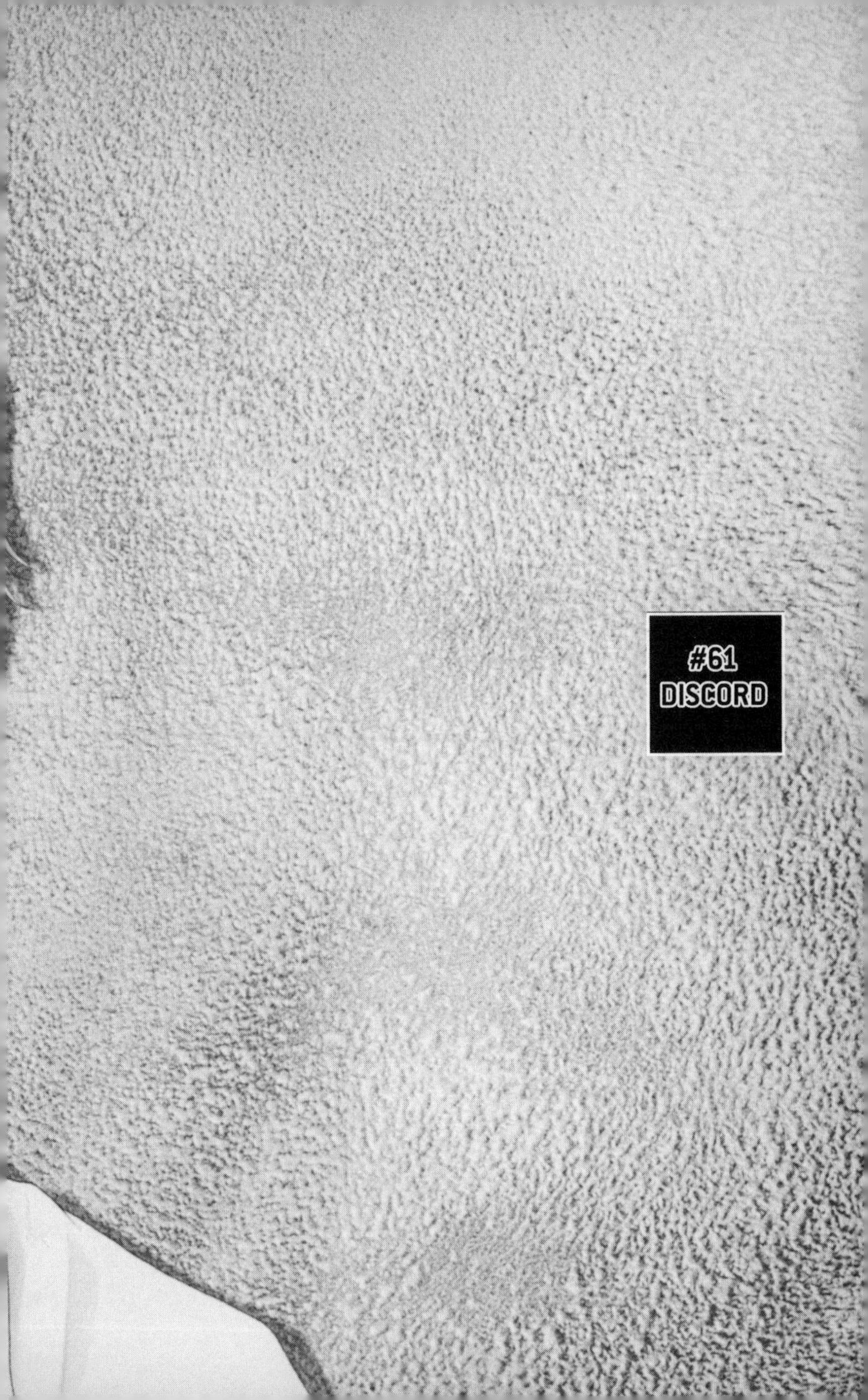

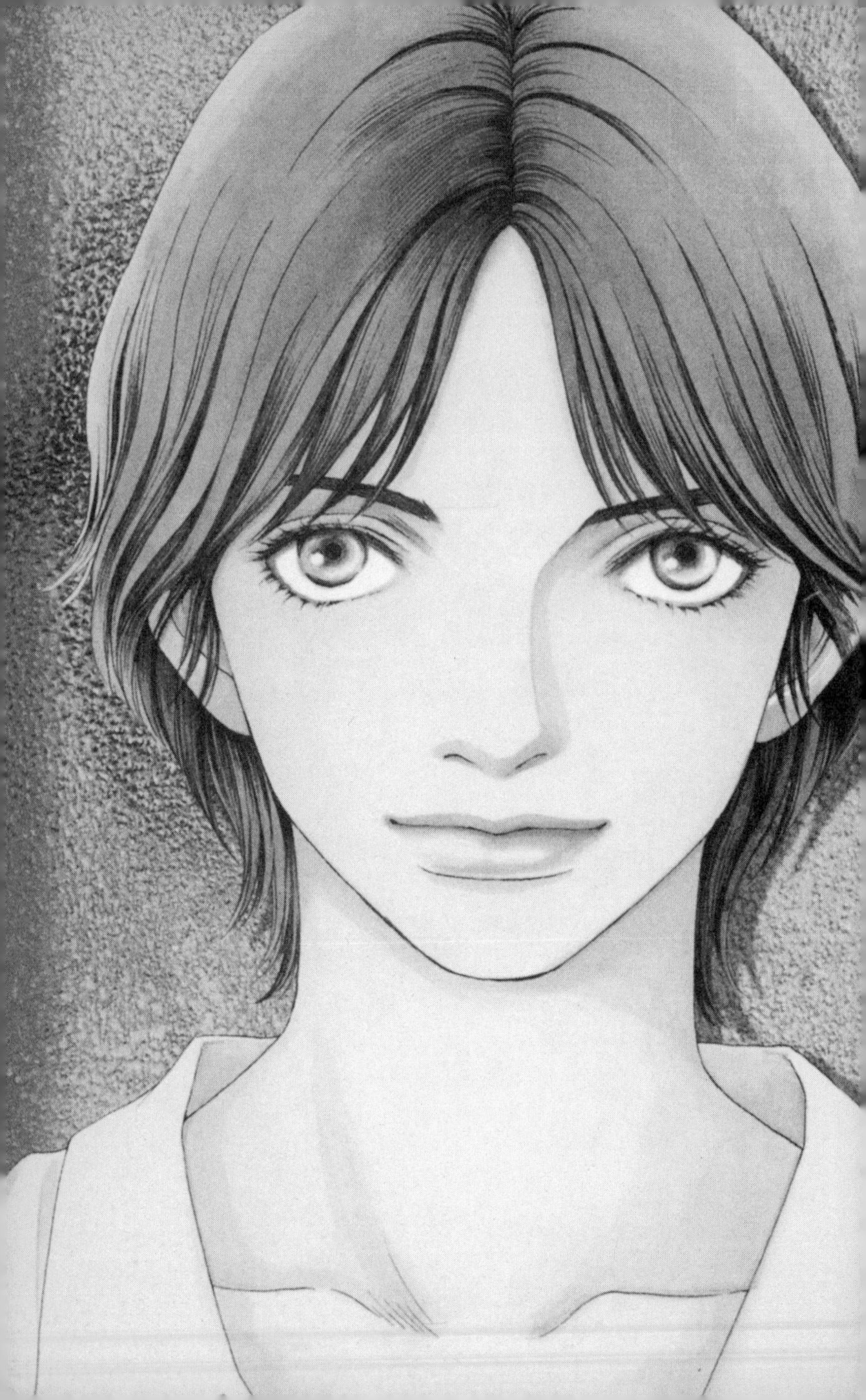

I've been waiting for you, Yuri.

Gimme back my stuff.
Tomo-kun, you came to my house the other day, didn't you?

I saw you leave my house.
What were you doing in there?
Did you do something to my mom and dad?
Only to your mom.

I was just gonna look for the gun you stole from me.
Your mom was home, so I figured I'd read her mind to see if she knew anything.
I found out that she's complete scum!
Did you know she killed the baby inside her body?

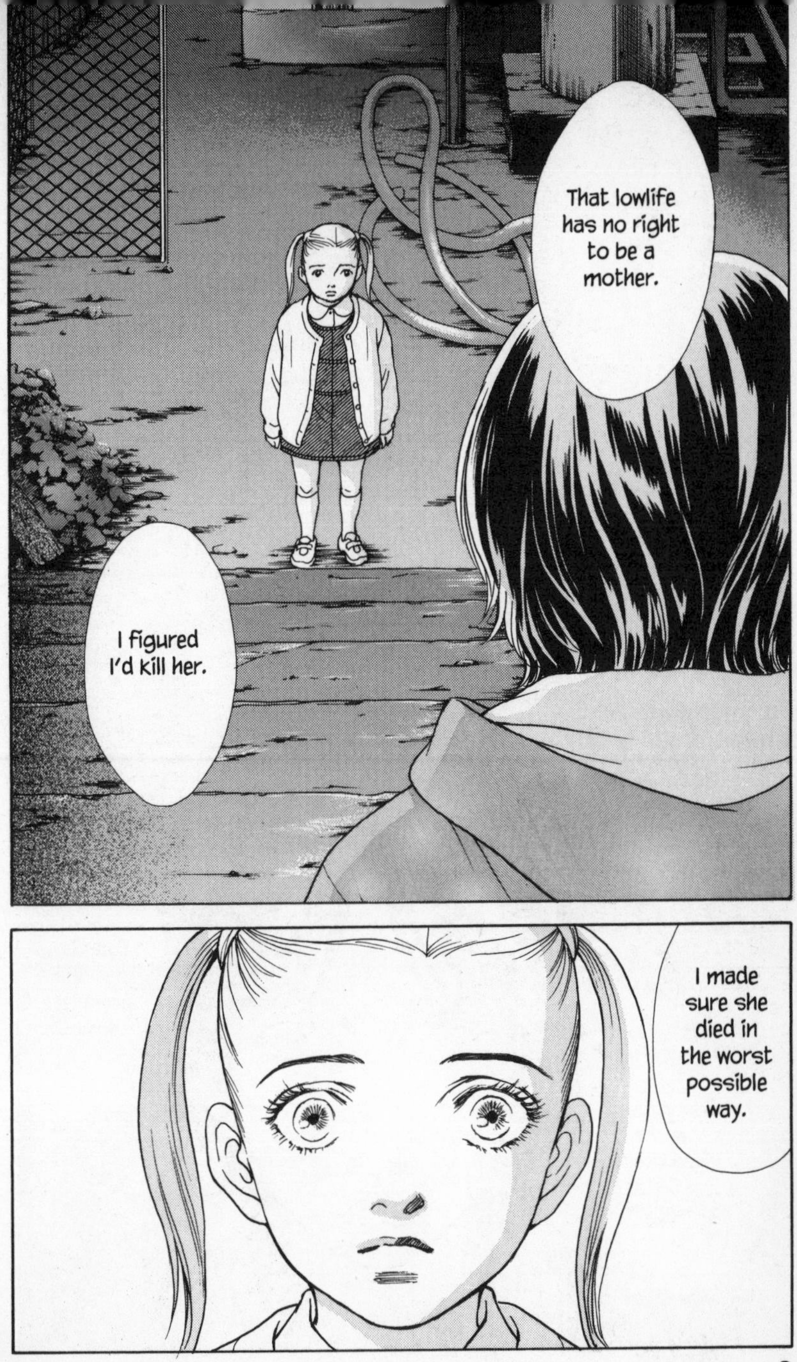
That lowlife has no right to be a mother.
I figured I'd kill her.
I made sure she died in the worst possible way.

Your mother gave up having a baby for you, Yuri.
She loved you, and she wanted to focus on you.
You...

You didn't have to do that!
You didn't have to kill Mommy!
Bring her back!

What the hell!
You said you didn't like her!
You're the one who said she didn't act like a real mom!
I got rid of her *for you!*

I didn't want you to *kill* her!
Why are you mad, Yuri?
I did all this for you!
You should be glad to be rid of her!
Right?
Don't touch me!!
THUD

THUD
I didn't like my mommy.
That doesn't mean I wanted her dead!
If she's dead, she can't apologize to me.
We can't become friends.
She can't learn to love me!

I want my mommy back!
Give her back to me!

RRRING
プルルル
RRRING
プルルル
Hello?
Yuri!
What's going on?
……

Tomo-
kun killed
Mommy.
Yuri,
you
saw...
You
were
with
Tomo-
kun?
Yeah...
The day my
mommy and
daddy died...
I
actually
saw...

...Tomo-kun leave my house.
I went to see him to make sure.
You went to meet him!?
Uh-huh.
I asked him if he did it and he said yes.
Yuri, where are you?
Near our secret meeting spot.
It's near that empty factory I showed you before.

Tomo-kun's a bad boy.
Kujyou-san, you were right.
Yuri, please...
Listen to me.
I want you to get away from there!
You have to get far away from Tomo-kun. Run!

#62
BRIDGE
Mommy!?

Yuri, I'm so sorry.
I've been so hard on you.
I'm going to be a good mother to you from now on.
I won't let you feel sad anymore.
Please forgive me.

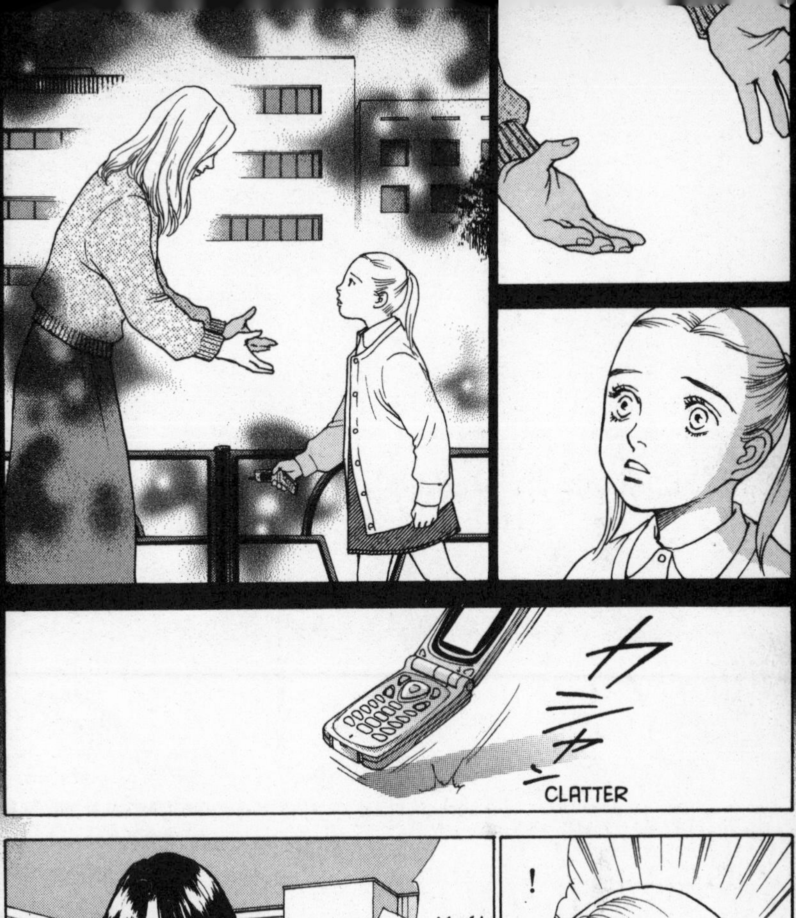
CLATTER
!
Yuri!
Yuri!

Hello? Hello!?
Yuri!!
SNAP
パチン

BEEP

Isaac's
got
Yuri...!

Where is she right now?
Her secret meeting place, she said.
Remem-ber that abandoned factory that Sakaki-san was called out to?
Let's go.
!
We have to help Yuri.
Hurry!

TUG
Akiba-kun, wait!

I'm really sorry, Yuri.
I made you suffer for a long time.
From now on, I promise to put you first.

We'll go to places you want to, like restaurants and amusement parks.
Yuri, your father and I will be with you all the time. We promise.
I thought you and daddy were dead?
That means you or daddy can't be with me anymore, right?
It's all right, Yuri. You're just going to have to come to me.

Come to you?
!

Mommy!
Wait!
Where are you going!?
Mommy!

I don't think she's around here anymore.
I'm sure Isaac is keeping close to Yuri.
I can't feel his presence around here.

She can't be too far away.
I could hear traffic in the background, so I'm sure she was facing the road.
The only place that gets a lot of traffic around here is that busy road with the bridge.
All right, we'll search over there.
Let's go!

Mommy!
Mommy, wait!
Mommy!

Mommy!

She has to be on that bridge.

#63
INTO THE
DARKNESS
I can feel
Isaac's
presence on
that bridge.

Come with me, Yuri. Let's go.
Mom!

Yuri!

Yuri!
SKREECH

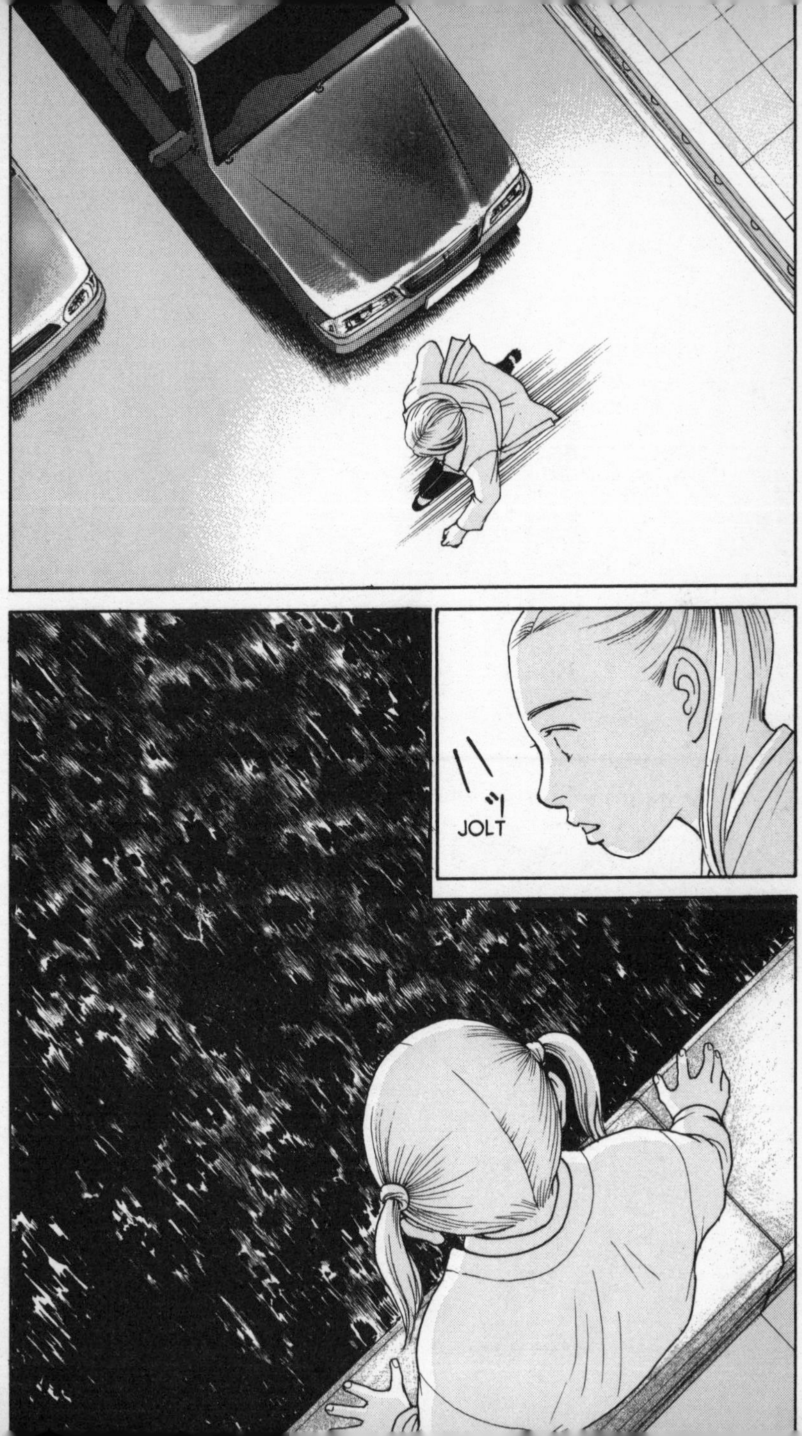
JOLT

WOBBLE
フラ…

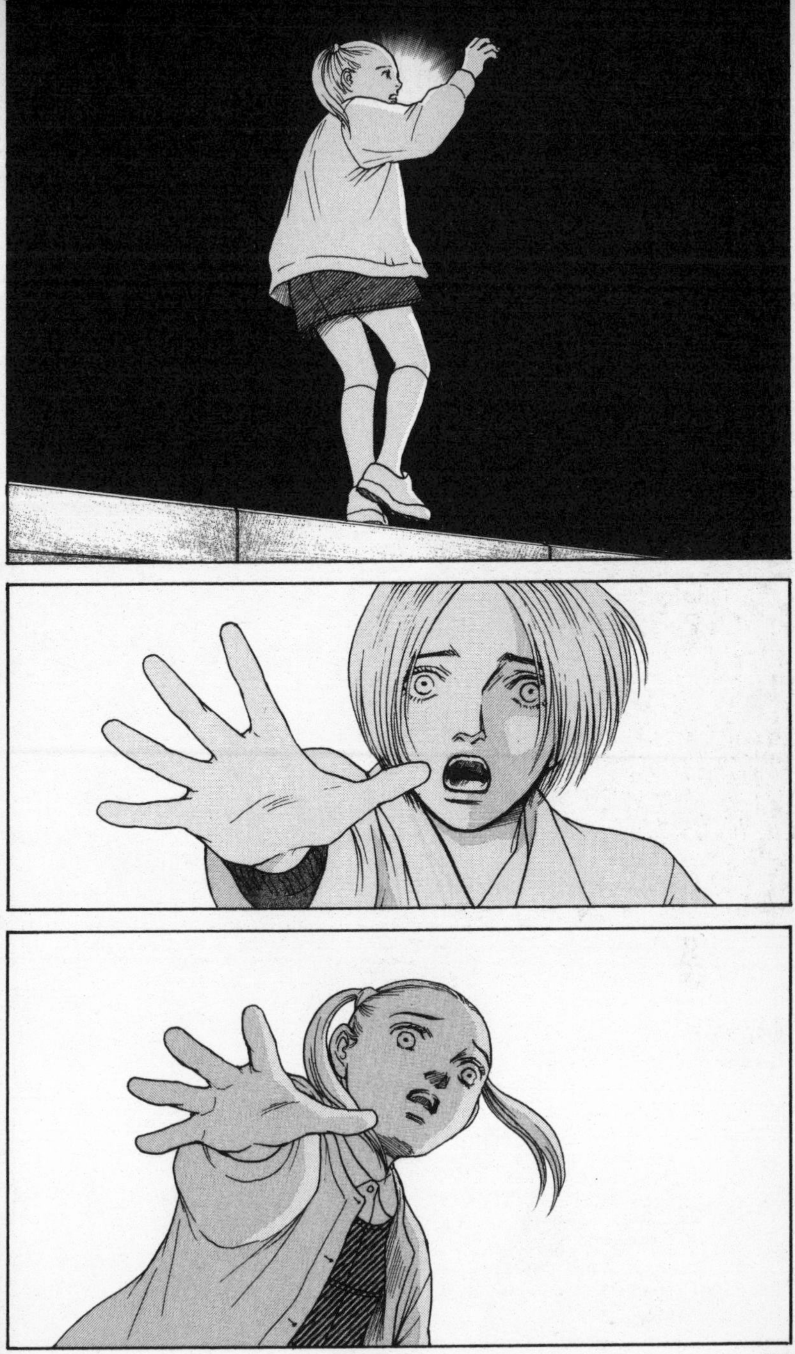

Mine-
san!

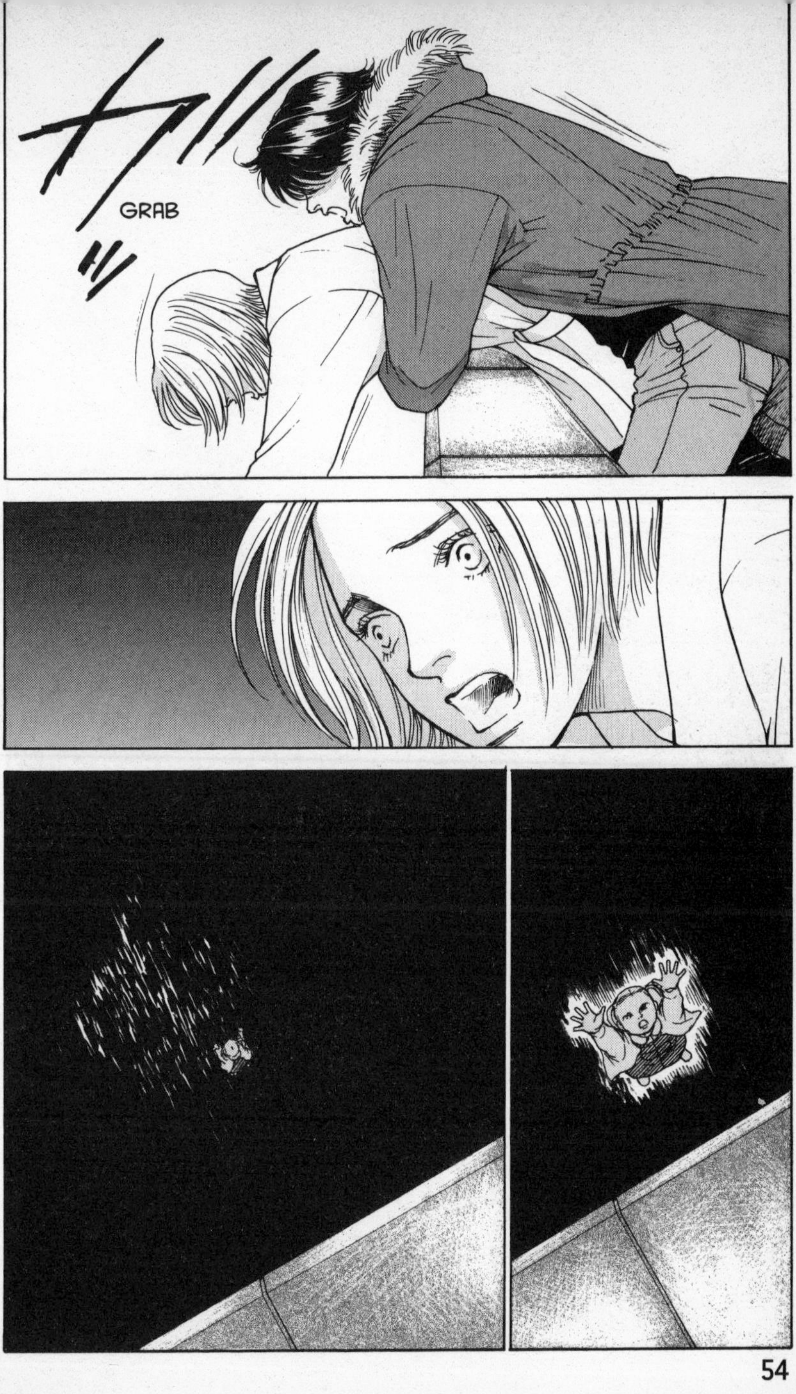
GRAB

NOOOO!

We found her!

——The end of #63 Into the Darkness——

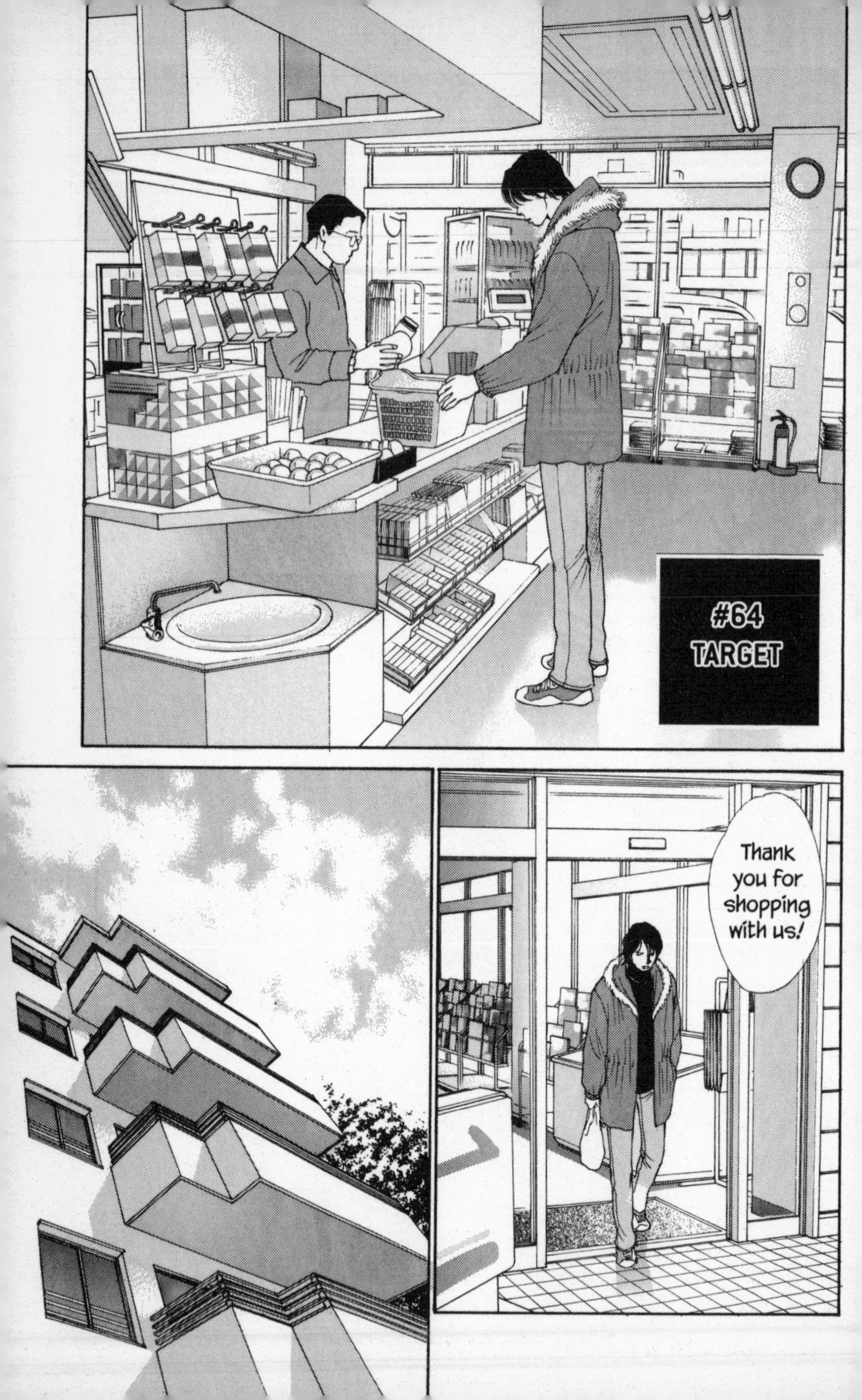
#64
TARGET
Thank you for shopping with us!

トン
THUMK
You really should eat some-thing.
Here, I bought some food.

This can't be good for your health.
You haven't eaten anything since last night!
You're going to collapse.
I don't care.
I don't care what happens anymore.

I don't need to exist.
It doesn't matter.
It really doesn't.
I wasn't able to help anyone.
Not Kimiko,
not Iwamura-san or Yuri.
I watched them die helplessly.
I killed them!

Wait...
They died because they knew me.
They died because of my involvement with Isaac.
They all died because of me.
They did nothing wrong.
They would still be alive if it wasn't for me...
I killed them!
Mine-san!

I always thought I could get my way
if I worked hard and believed in myself.
There are certain things that I can't control,
no matter how hard I try.

This must be divine punish-ment.
Punish-ment?
God is punish-ing me for my ignorance and arrogance.
I don't think anyone can stop Isaac.
Mere humans can only grovel in the presence of an ES.

We'll just have to wait patiently
for the day when Isaac will kill us.

キイ
CREAK
PA-TAN
パタン

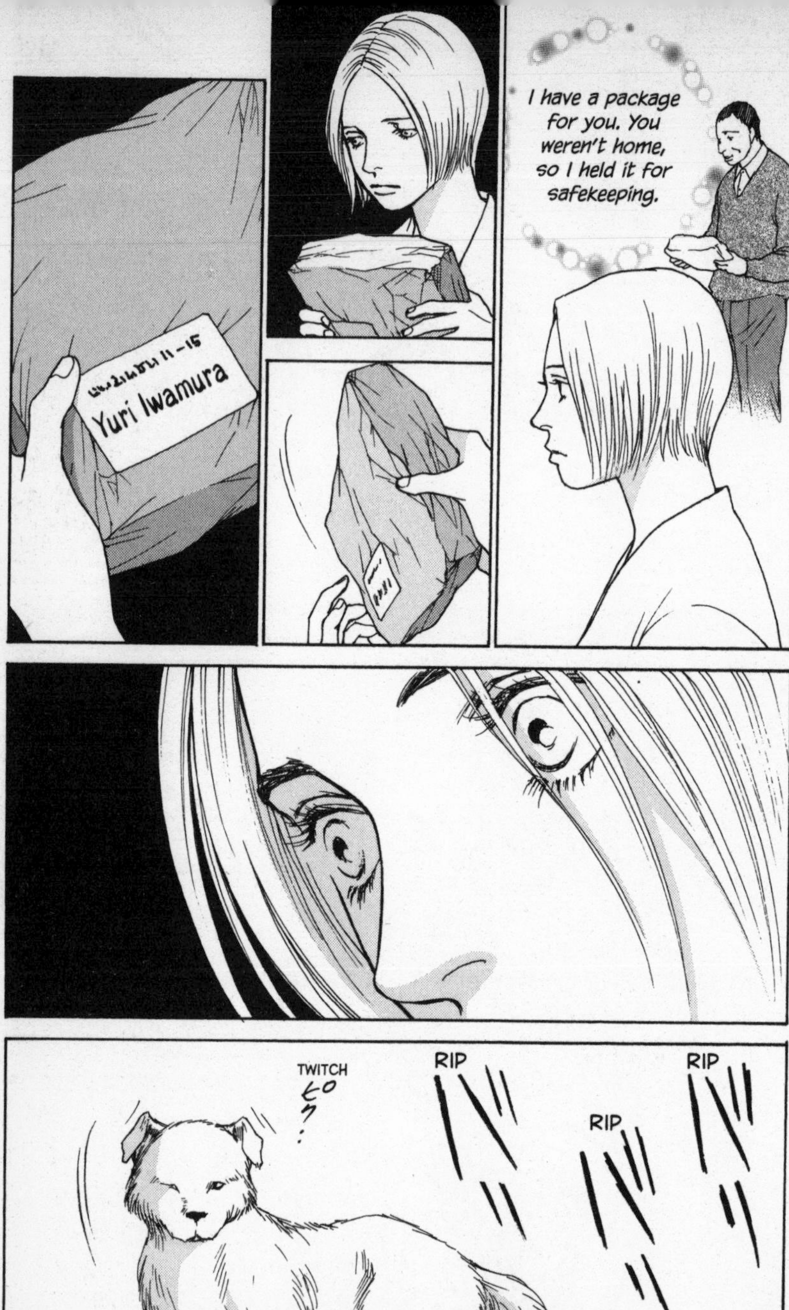
I have a package for you. You weren't home, so I held it for safekeeping.
Yuri Iwamura
RIP
RIP
RIP
TWITCH

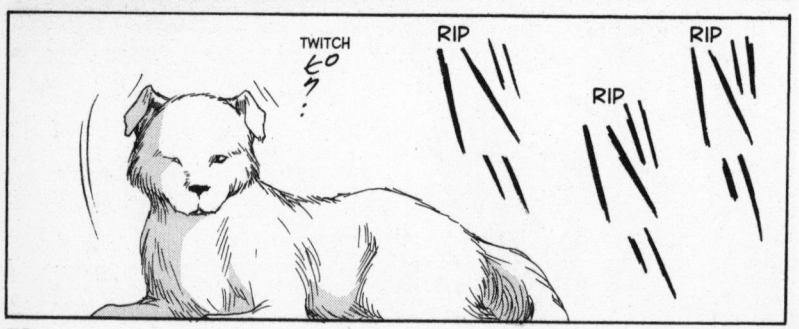

Mine-san?
Mine-san!?

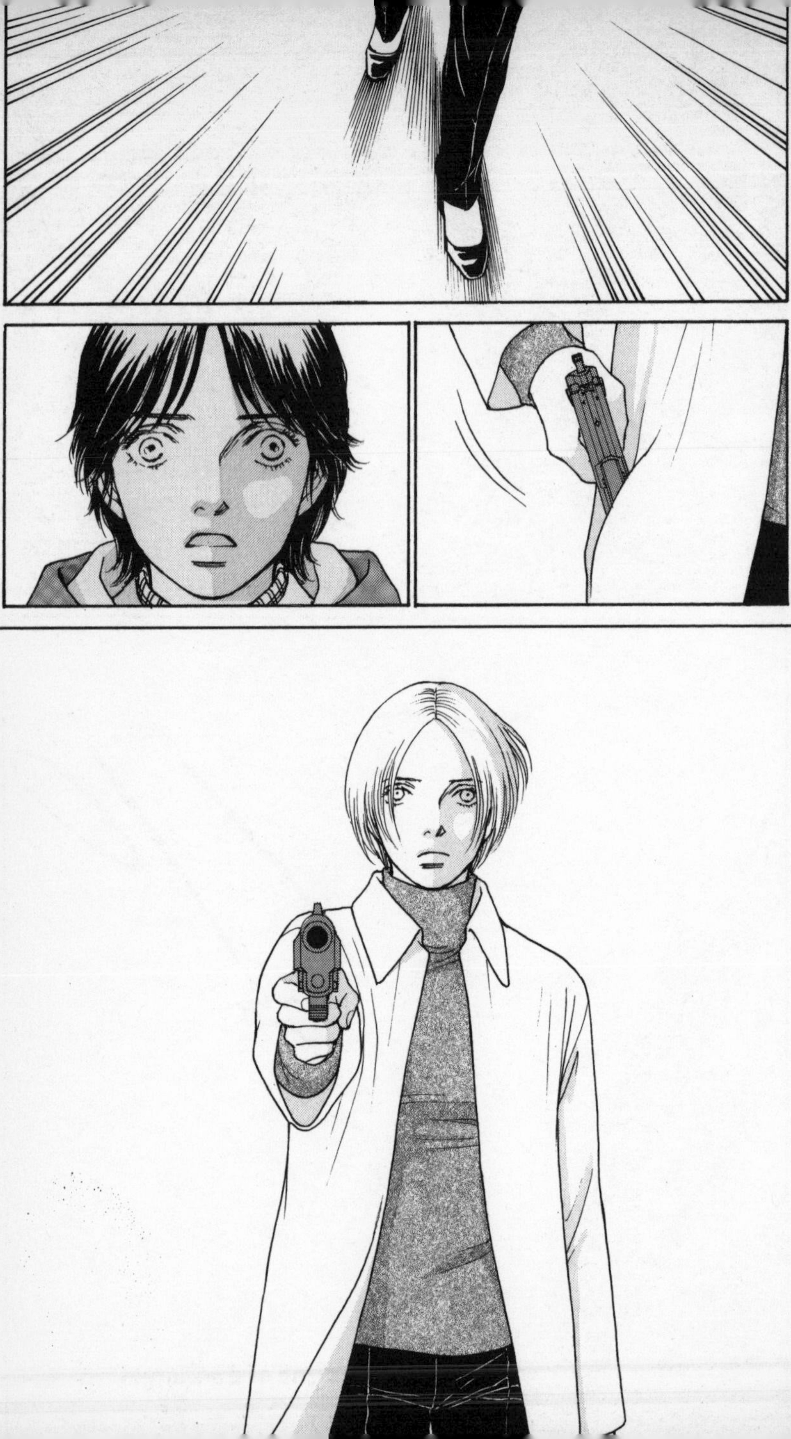

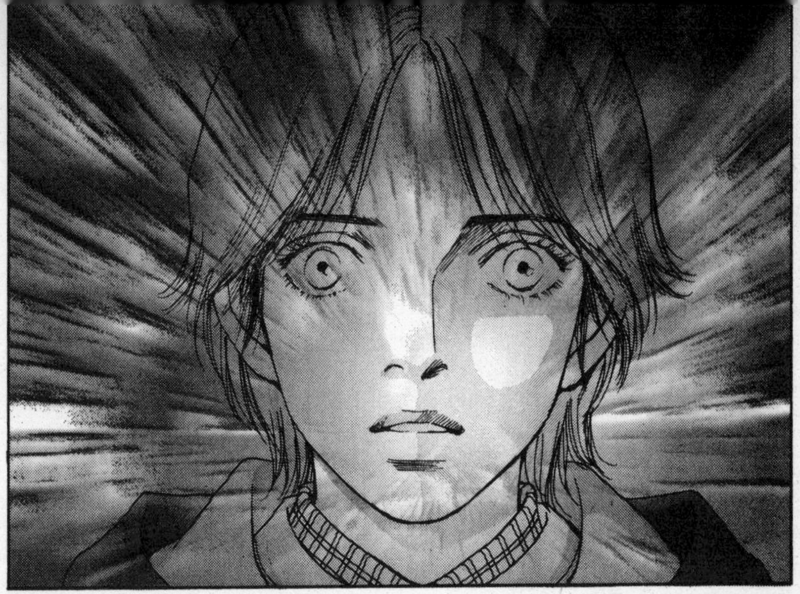

20

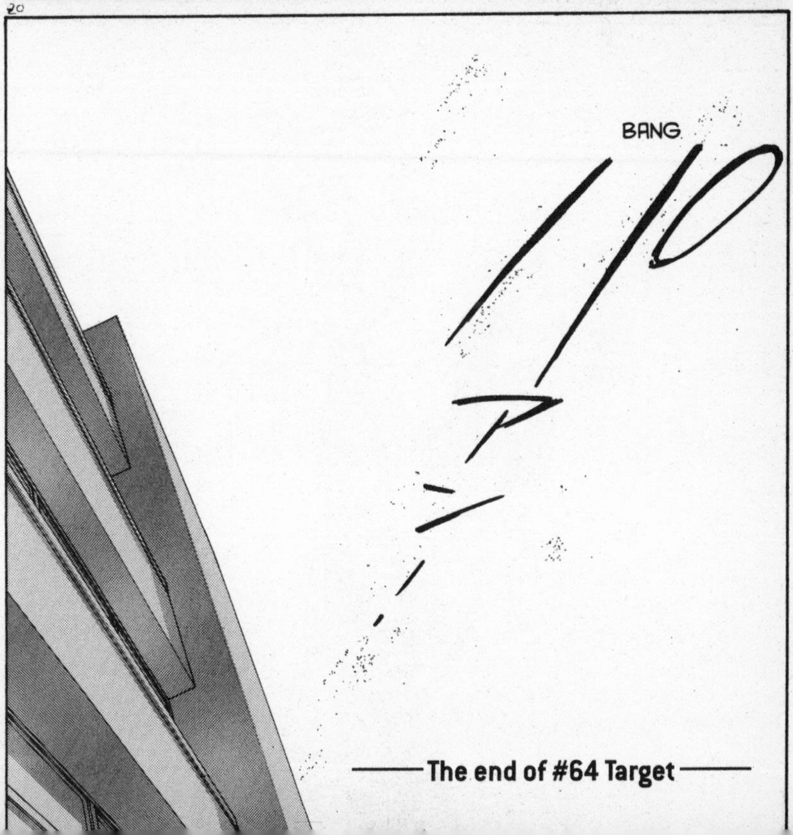
BANG
—The end of #64 Target—

#65
LINE OF FIRE,
PART I

POP
CRACK
!

Freeze, dammit!
Isaac!
JERK
ハッ
!

PSHHHTTTT

KOFF
ゲホ
KOFF
ゲホ
It's just tear gas. It won't cause permanent damage.
I'm sorry!

PANT
はあ
PANT
はあ・・
PANT
はあ・・

Isaac!
You're not getting away with what you did!

BANG
SPLAT
SLAM
GYAAAH!
PANT
PANT
No...

Murderer!
You god-damned murderer!!!
Remember that! You pull that trigger and you're nothing but a killer!
I'm glad I learned to shoot a gun when I lived in the United States.

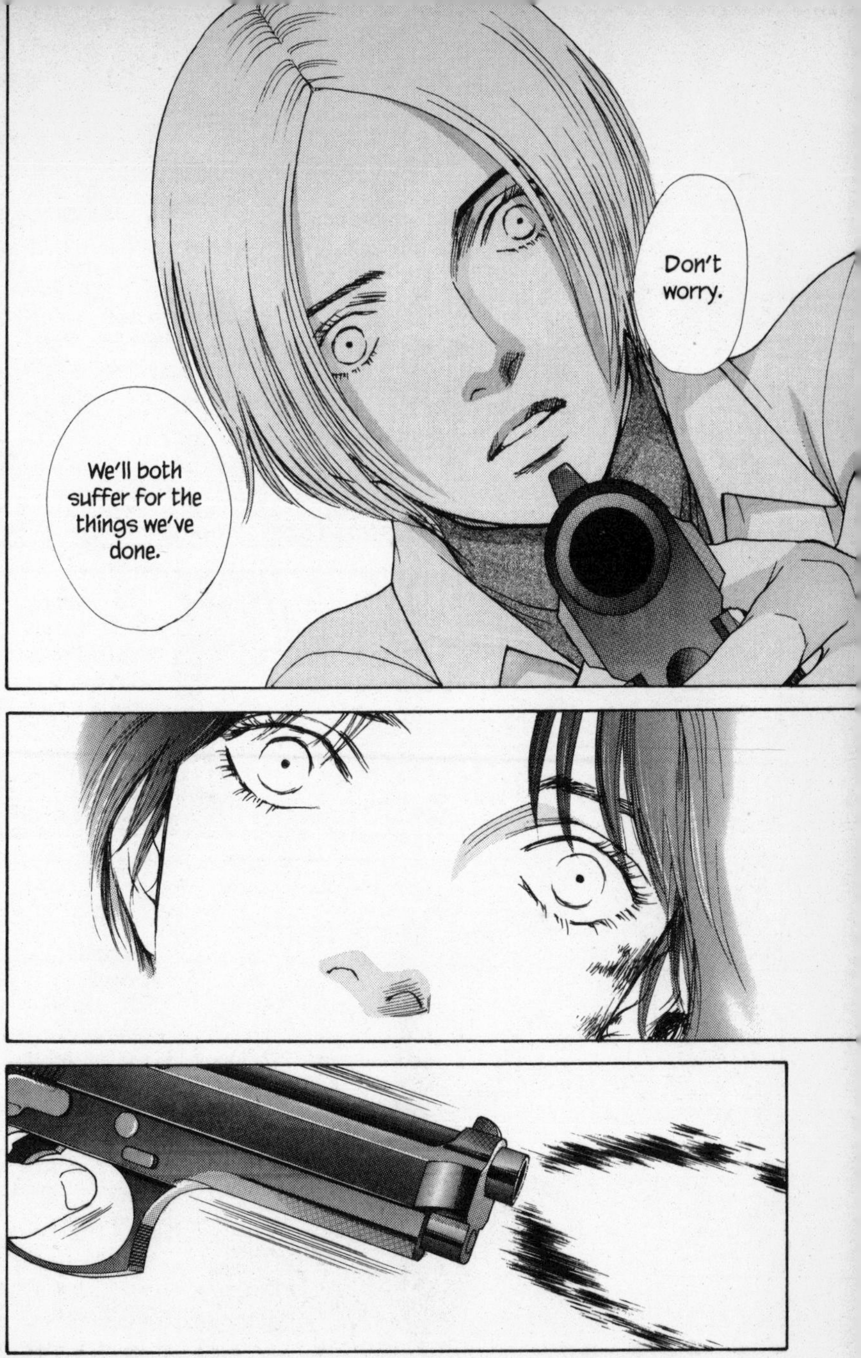
Don't worry.
We'll both suffer for the things we've done.

GUAAAHHH!

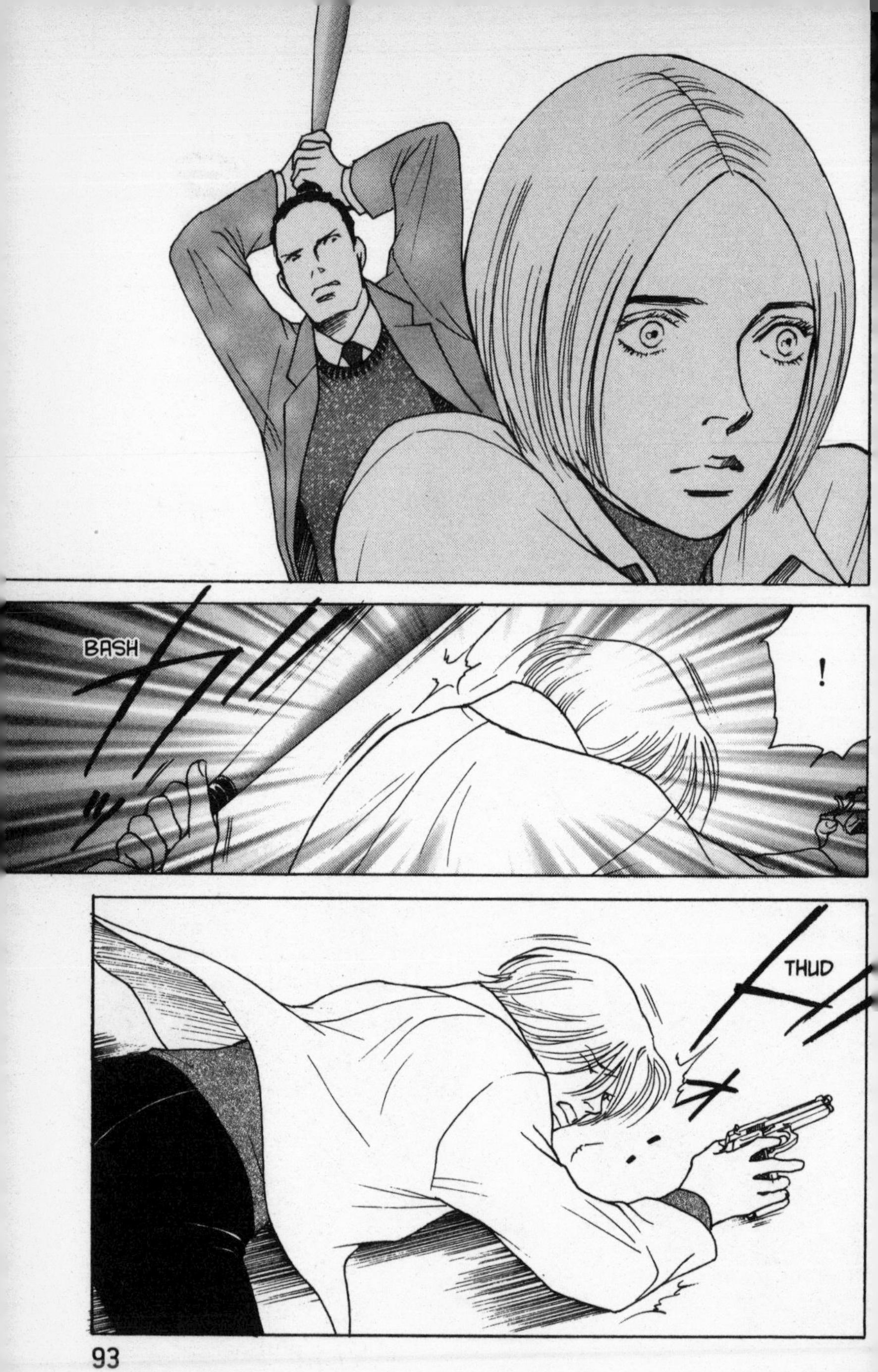
BASH
!
THUD

Unh...

ガッ KICK

Too bad you failed, Mine Kujyou.
I admit you've got balls, lady.

CLICK
カチッ
CLICK
カチッ
CLICK
カチッ
Isaac!

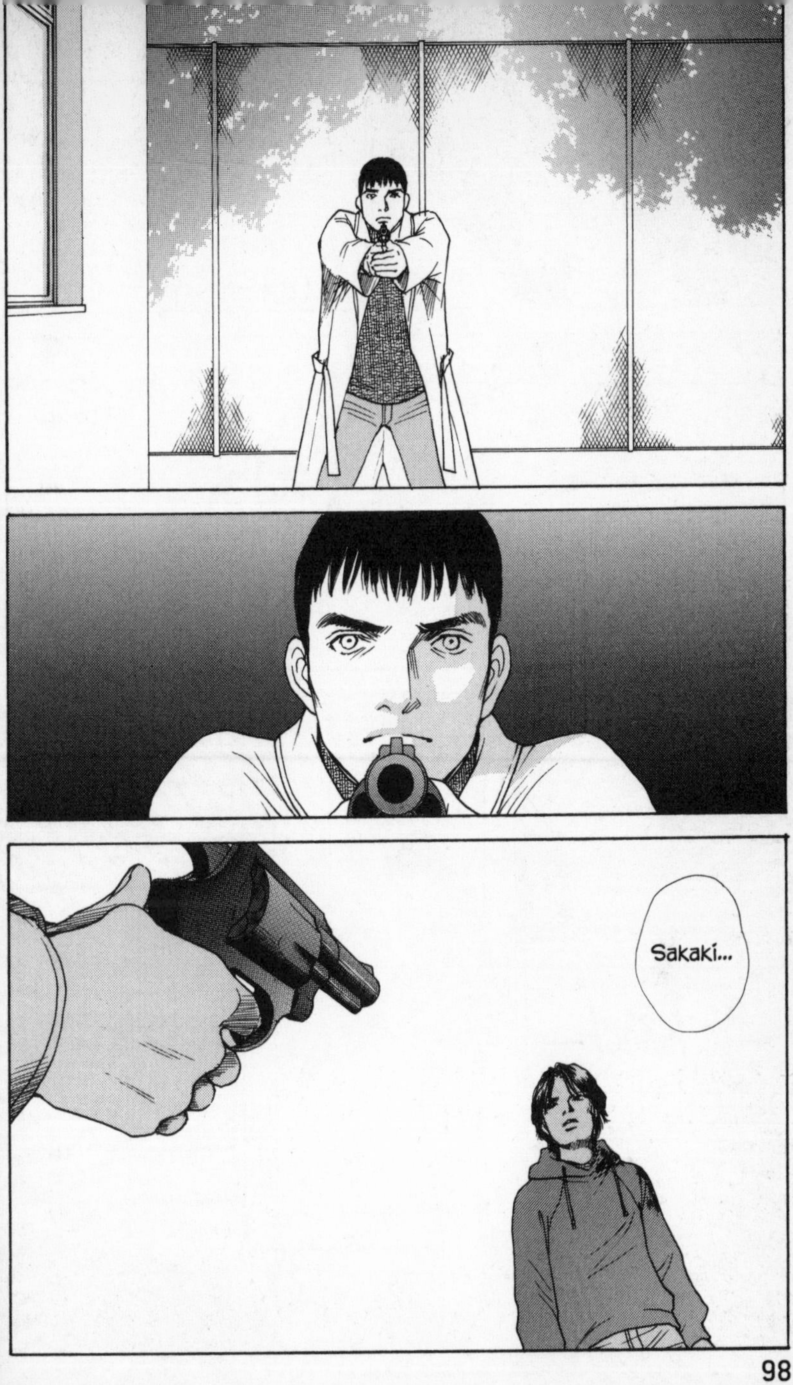
Sakaki...

ヨロ ヨロ…
STAGGER
SWING
スッ
!

The end of #65 Line of Fire, Part I

#66
LINE OF FIRE,
PART II

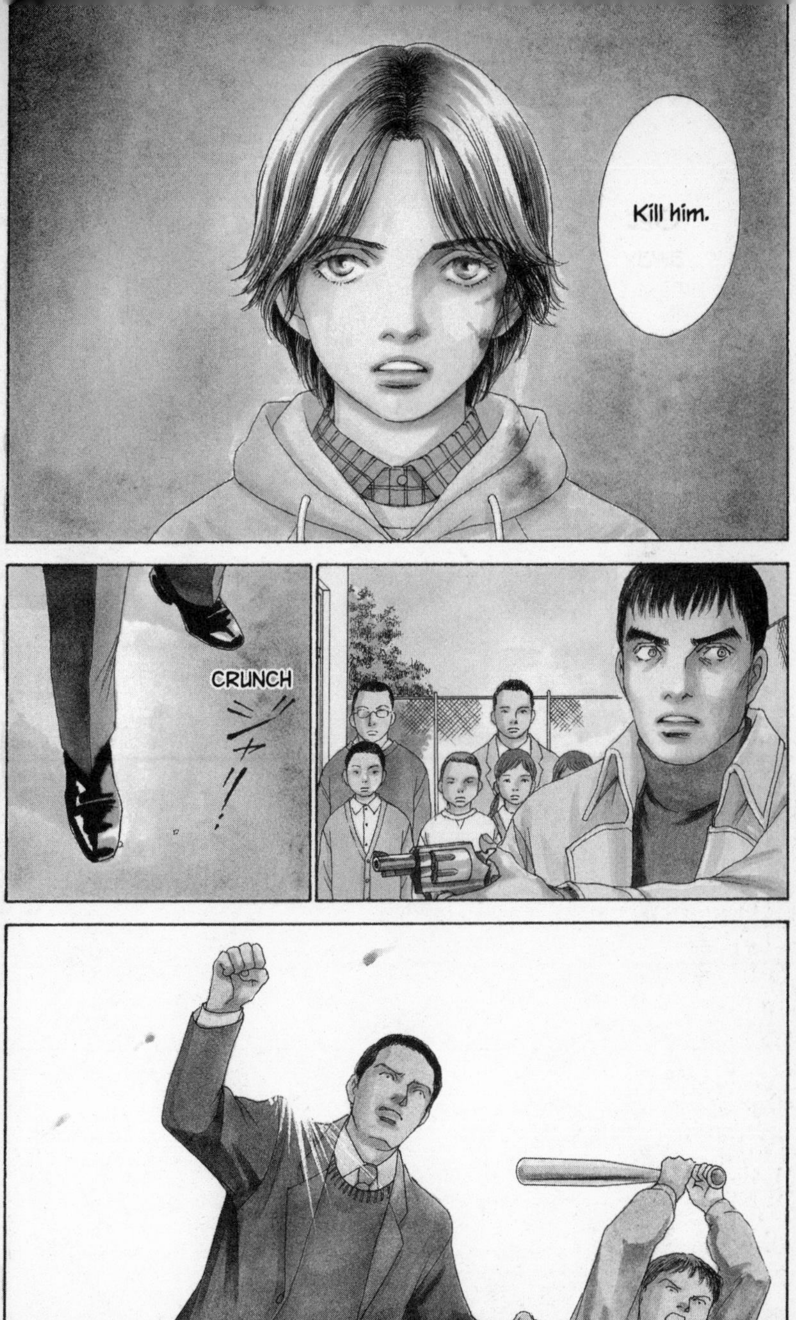
Kill him.
CRUNCH

Get away from me!

Shuro!

RATTLE

!
Shuro!
I've been waiting for you!
Grab Mine right now!

!
Are you sure you won't need it later?
I'm sure. It's not real.
CHUCK
Let's toss that.
It was only a bluff to help me buy time until you showed up.

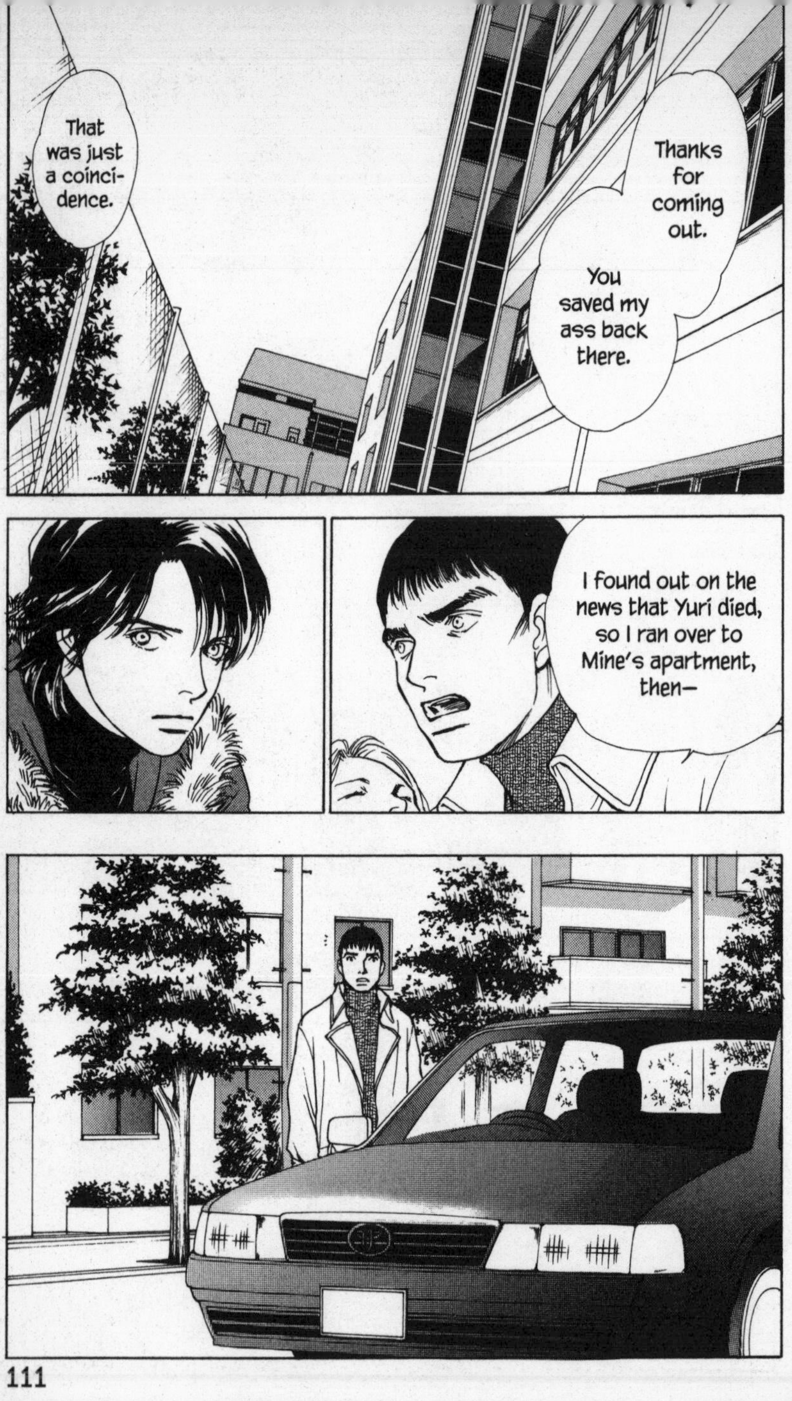
Thanks for coming out.
You saved my ass back there.
That was just a coinci-dence.
I found out on the news that Yuri died, so I ran over to Mine's apartment, then—

I got worried and chased after her. I was surprised to see her stop at Isaac's school.
I freaked out and called you on your cell.

Either way, I had new information for both you and Mine.
I never thought I'd see you under these circum-stances.
It seems like we always find you when I least expect it.
Look, it's the same deal again.
!

Isaac...

They are my soldiers.
You're not getting out of here alive!
Slaugh-ter them!
Tear them to pieces!

So you want to play war games?

SNAP

And so begins our fight to the death.

—The end of #66 Line of Fire, Part II—

He's...
...dead?
I had no choice.
He would have killed us otherwise.

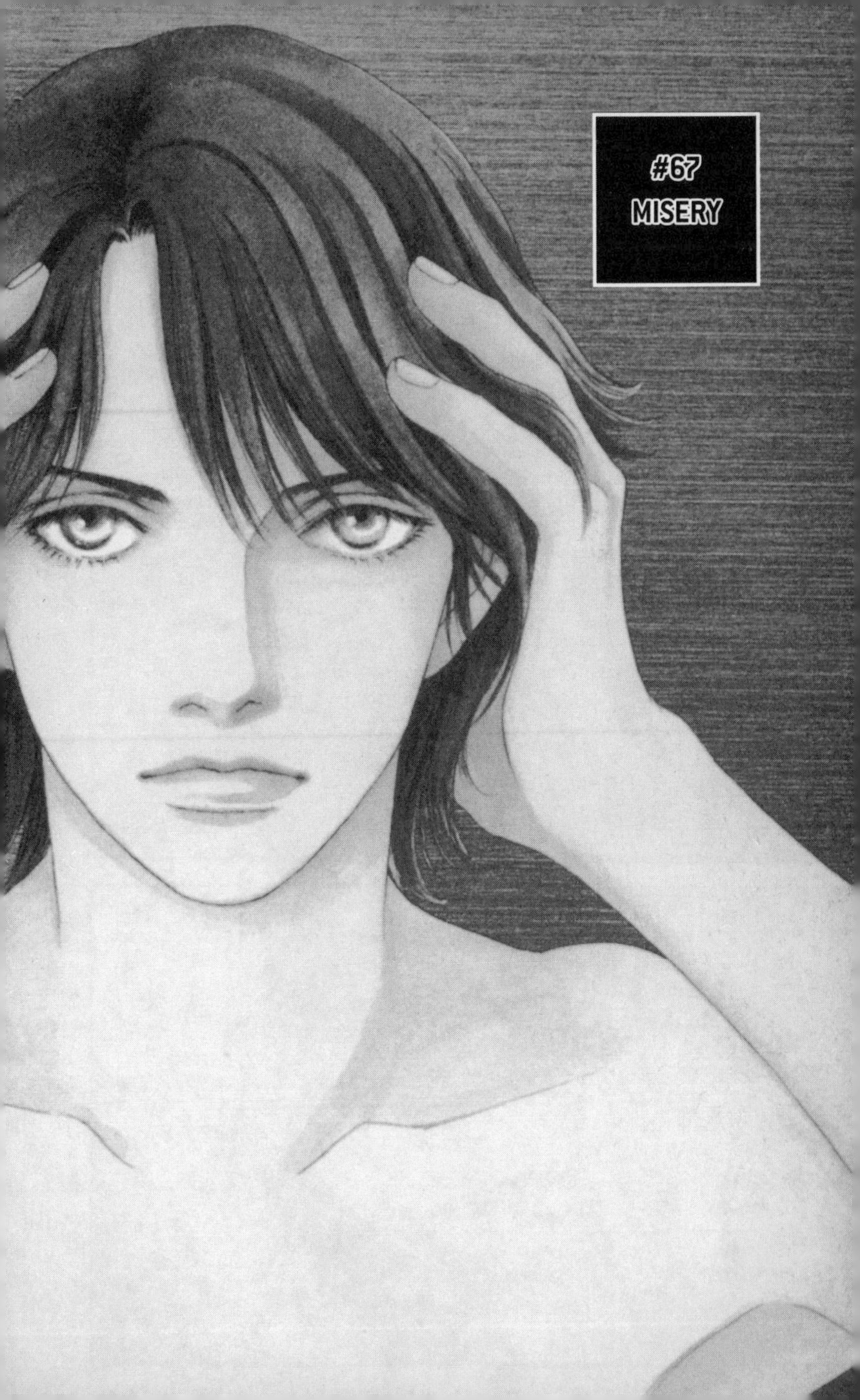
#67
MISERY

They're not going to get away.

We have to run.
Take Mine to your car!
!
STAGGER
ヨロ
ヨロッ
STAGGER

GYAAH!
!
Shuro! Hurry up!
UGHHHH!
Don't worry about me. Get Mine to a safe place!

VRRRROAR
ブロロロ…

Move it!
Out of my way!
BUMP

Get in! Hurry!
Shuro!
JOLT
DASH

Yuri!
JOLT
ッ

!
カッ
CHOKE
Shuro!

Shuro...
You're dead meat.
Shurrr-ooooo!
Just go! Move!
Now!
Kill him!

Kill him!

Shuro!

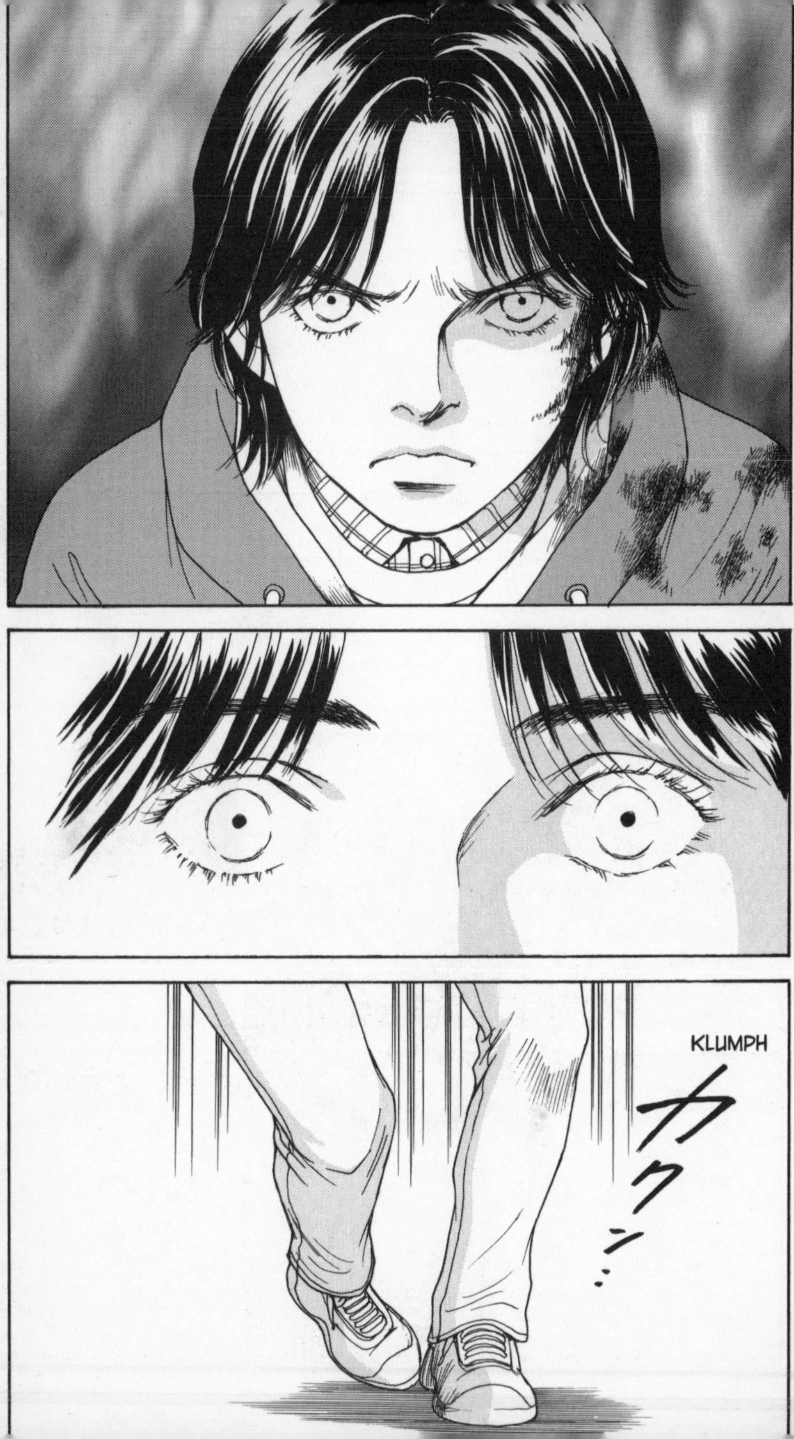
KLUMPH
カクン…

THUD
What?
JOLT

Shuro, this is your chance! Get in!
DASH
Let's get out of here!

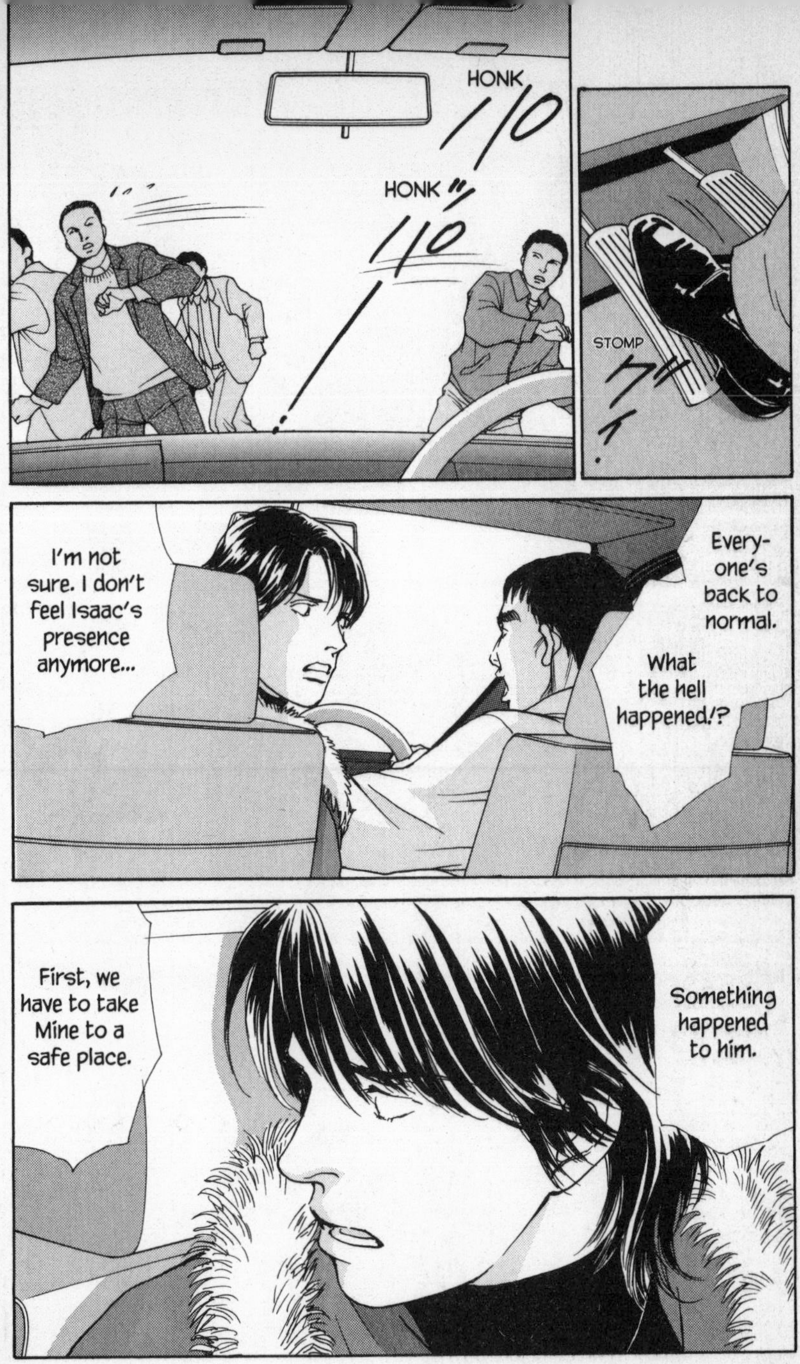
STOMP
HONK
HONK
Every-one's back to normal.
What the hell happened!?
I'm not sure. I don't feel Isaac's presence anymore...
Something happened to him.
First, we have to take Mine to a safe place.

—The end of #67 Misery—

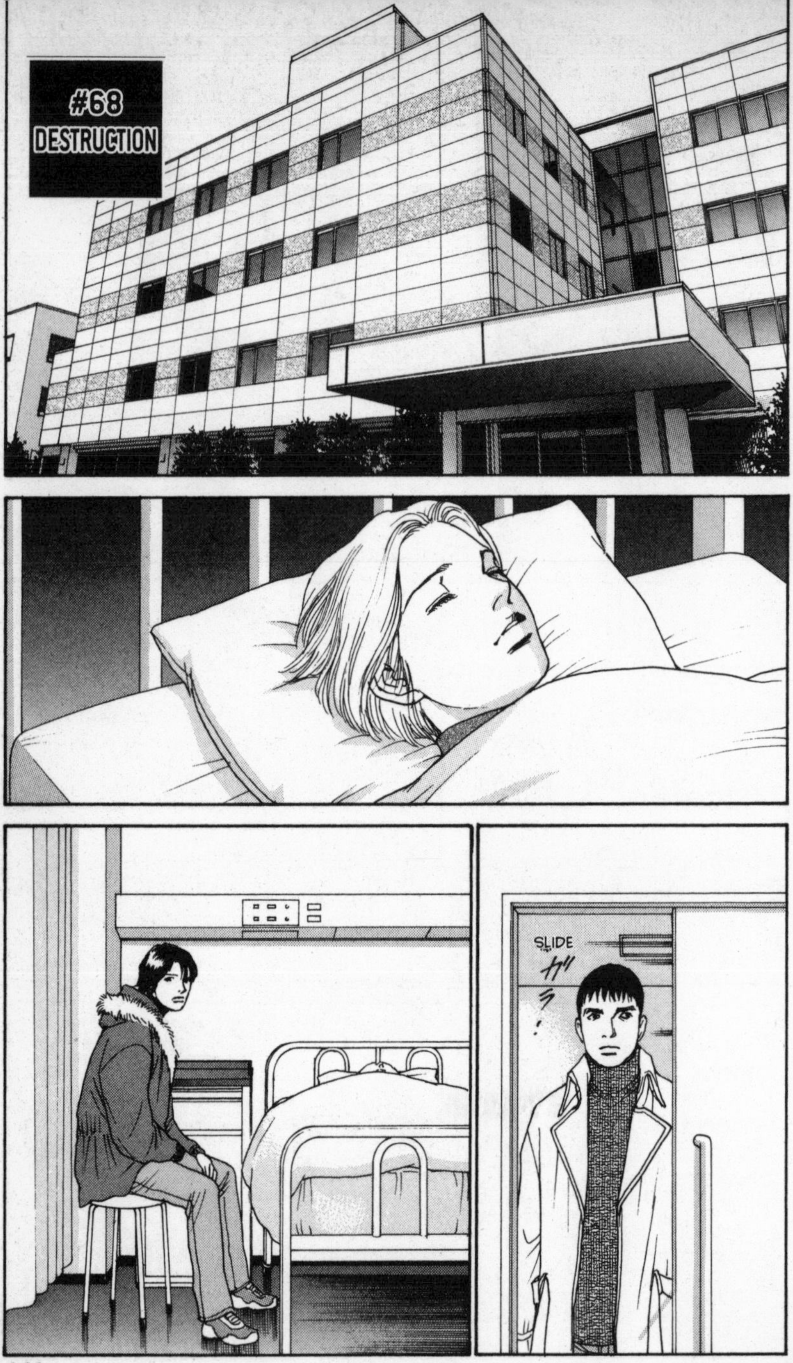
#68
DESTRUCTION
SLIDE
ガ
ラ

How is she doing?
She's in stable condition. She lost conscious-ness due to the impact.
They want to keep her overnight for observation.
I see...
Have you noticed any changes outside?
It's a huge mess. Looks like someone disturbed a hornet's nest.

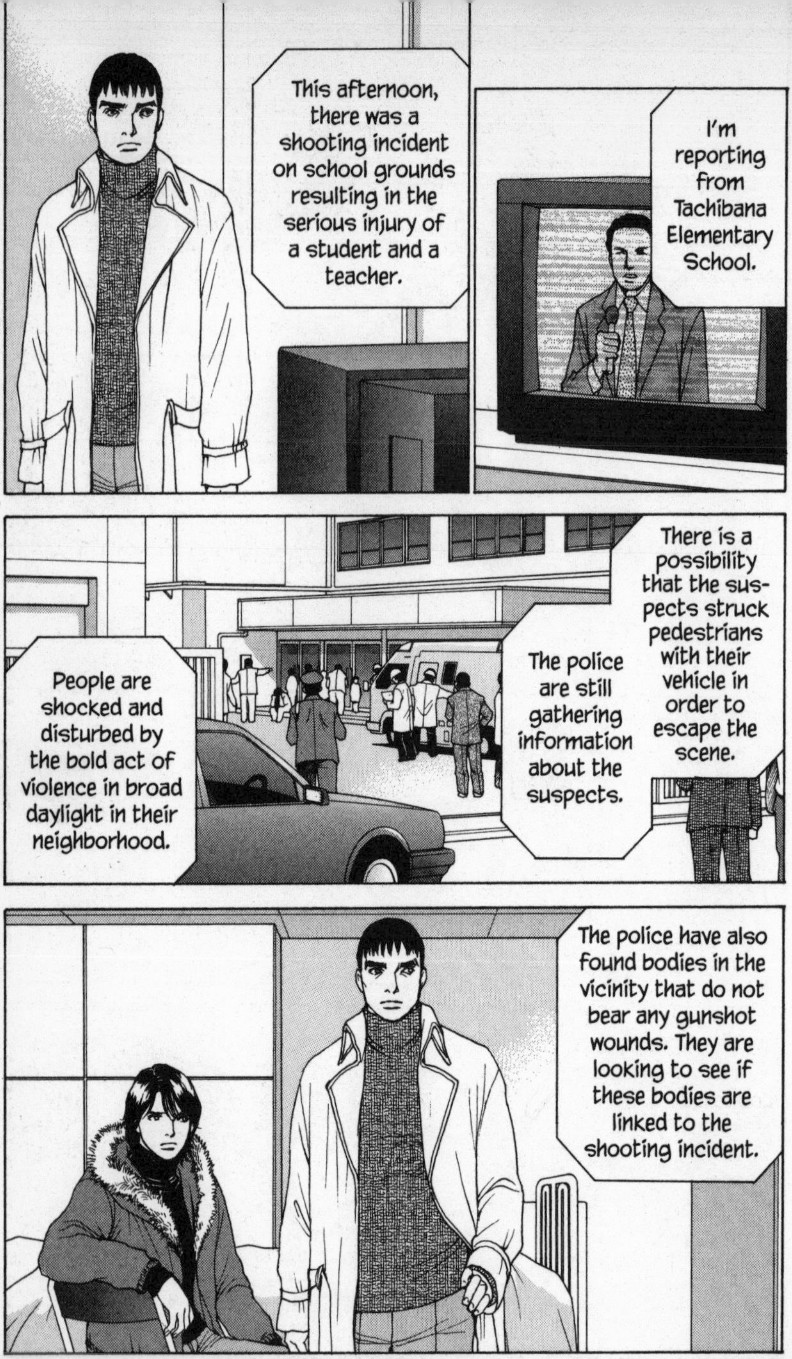
This afternoon, there was a shooting incident on school grounds resulting in the serious injury of a student and a teacher.
I'm reporting from Tachibana Elementary School.
There is a possibility that the suspects struck pedestrians with their vehicle in order to escape the scene.
The police are still gathering information about the suspects.
People are shocked and disturbed by the bold act of violence in broad daylight in their neighborhood.
The police have also found bodies in the vicinity that do not bear any gunshot wounds. They are looking to see if these bodies are linked to the shooting incident.

BLIP
This is the worst possible situation.
There was no way around it, if you ask me.
I'm just glad there were fewer victims than I expected.

I felt a sudden disconnect.
Isaac's presence just disappeared.
I don't get it...
This incredible violent frenzy also evaporated into thin air...
Did he change his mind, or did something happen to him?
......
I can't believe something happened to Isaac!
That can't be!

What if something did happen to him?
How?
What do you mean?
I've been holed up in a friend's lab for the last few weeks to analyze Isaac's blood sample one more time.

Re-examine Isaac's blood?
What for?
Kujyou-san was talking about the possibility of a weak-ness.
If Isaac is a clone of Akiba-kun, then is he a complete copy?
Weak-ness?
She feels that people with the same genes develop differences when exposed to disparate growth environments.
I studied his blood sample very carefully.

Did you discover anything?
Isaac is going to die very soon.

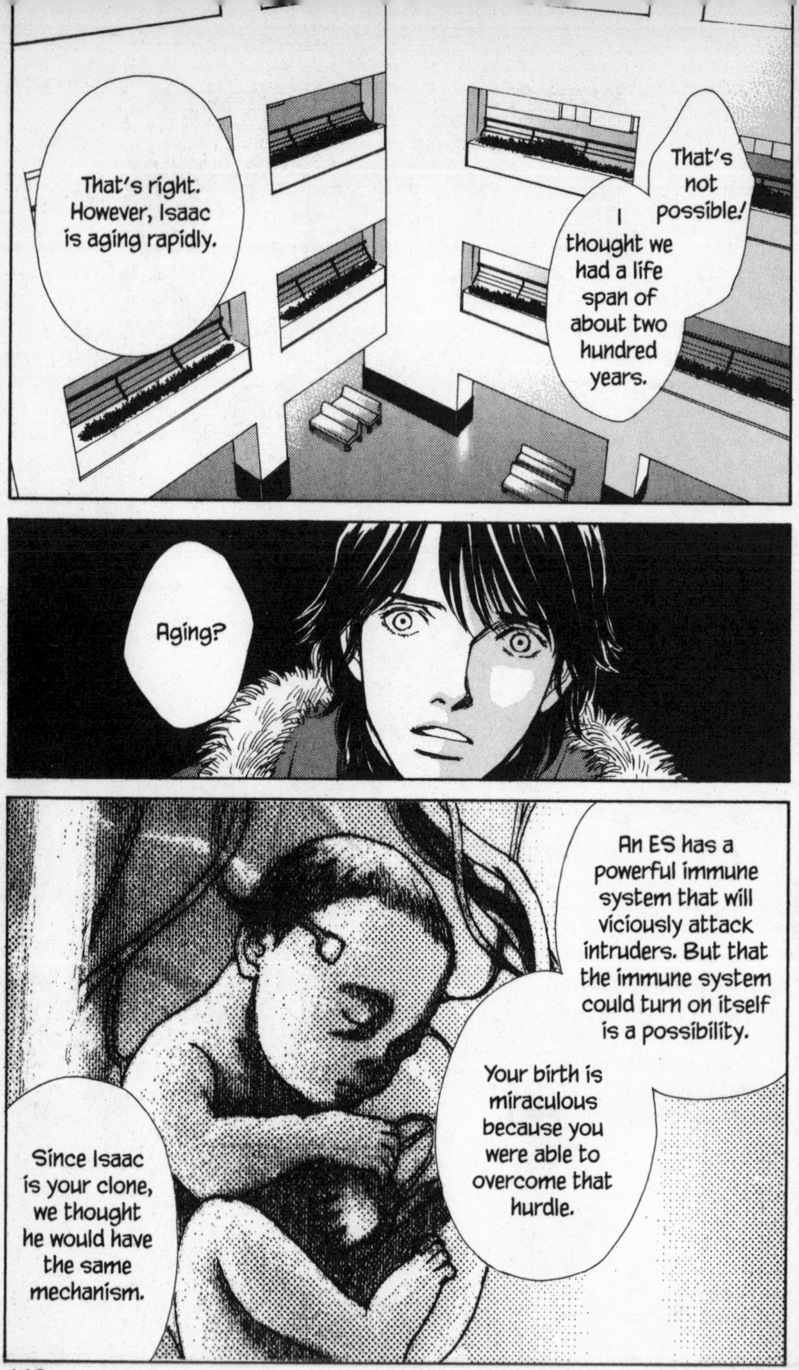
That's right. However, Isaac is aging rapidly.
That's not possible!
I thought we had a life span of about two hundred years.
Aging?
An ES has a powerful immune system that will viciously attack intruders. But that the immune system could turn on itself is a possibility.
Your birth is miraculous because you were able to overcome that hurdle.
Since Isaac is your clone, we thought he would have the same mechanism.

What went wrong?
It must have had an external cause.
Isaac was protected inside an artificial womb. He was exposed to the outside world rather suddenly.
Unlike you, he was not exposed in gradual steps.
That means he was suddenly exposed to a hostile environment full of airborne bacteria, micro-organisms, harmful chemicals, radiation...
His immune system must have been working overtime to compensate.

The immune system can be a double-edged sword.
The sudden exposure to the elements was too much, even for an ES.
The overcompensation took its toll in the form of accelerated aging that will rapidly advance in the next few months.
This is the end. He'll perish on his own.

I think we're on our way to a happy ending, although there were many victims along the way.
Either way, it looks like we won't have to kill Isaac.

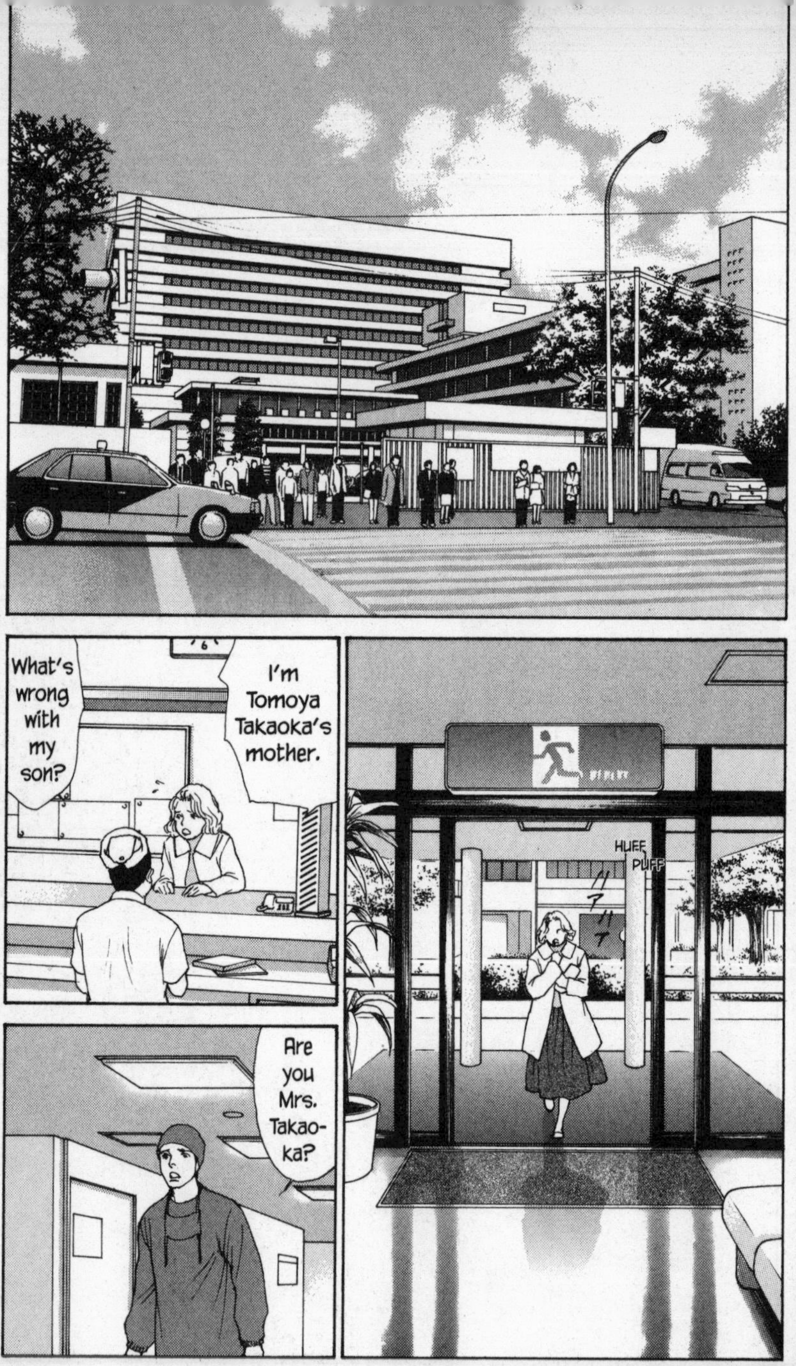
HUFF
PUFF
I'm Tomoya Takaoka's mother.
What's wrong with my son?
Are you Mrs. Takaoka?

NURSE STATION
Your son is in stable condition.
We were able to extract the bullet from his shoulder.
He will have a scar on the ear, but he's doing quite well.
The major problem is not his gunshot wound.
?

Tomo-kun!
No!
KYAAAAH!

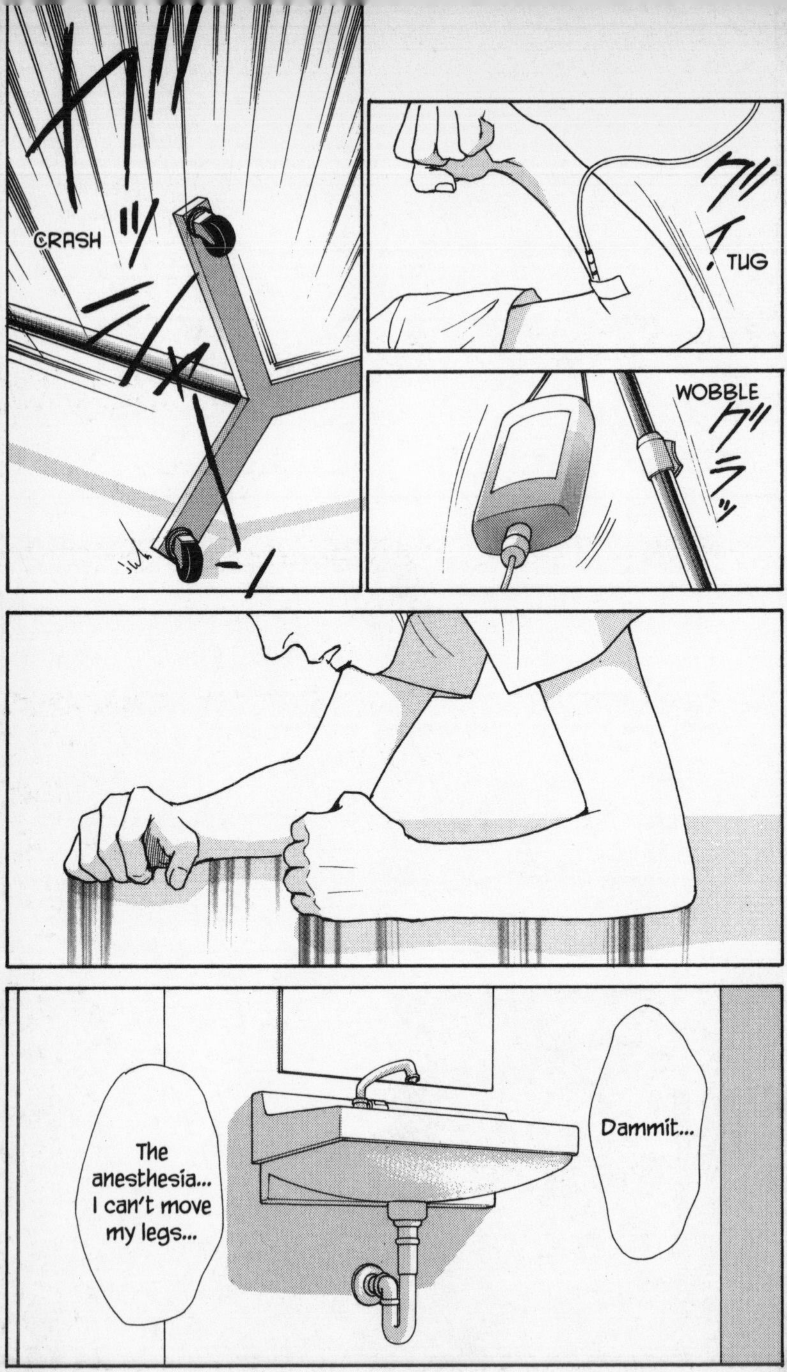
TUG
WOBBLE
CRASH
Dammit...
The anesthesia... I can't move my legs...

I feel like an invalid!
What a joke!

GRABB
What's going on!
What happened to my hair!
The end of #68 Destruction

Why do I have white hair!?
Why!?
#69 DECLINE
What's happening to me?
Why is this happening!?

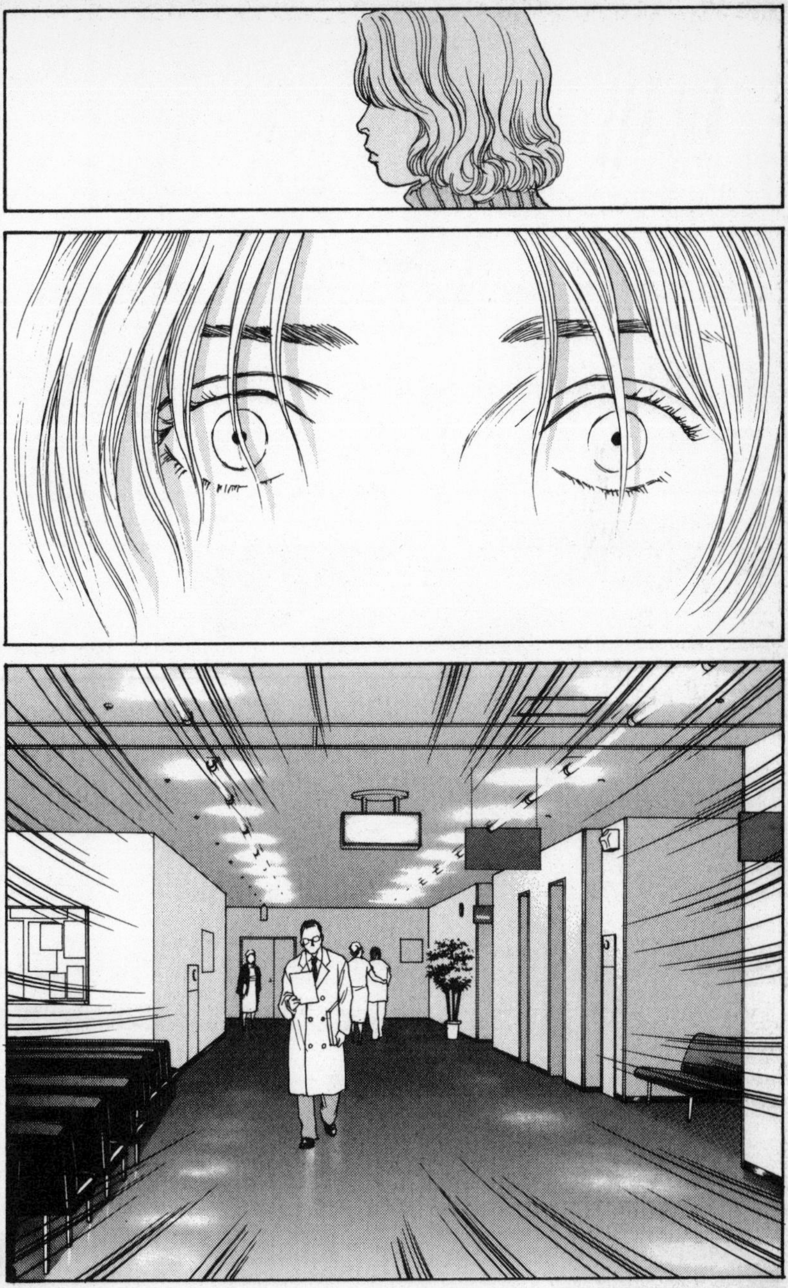

7

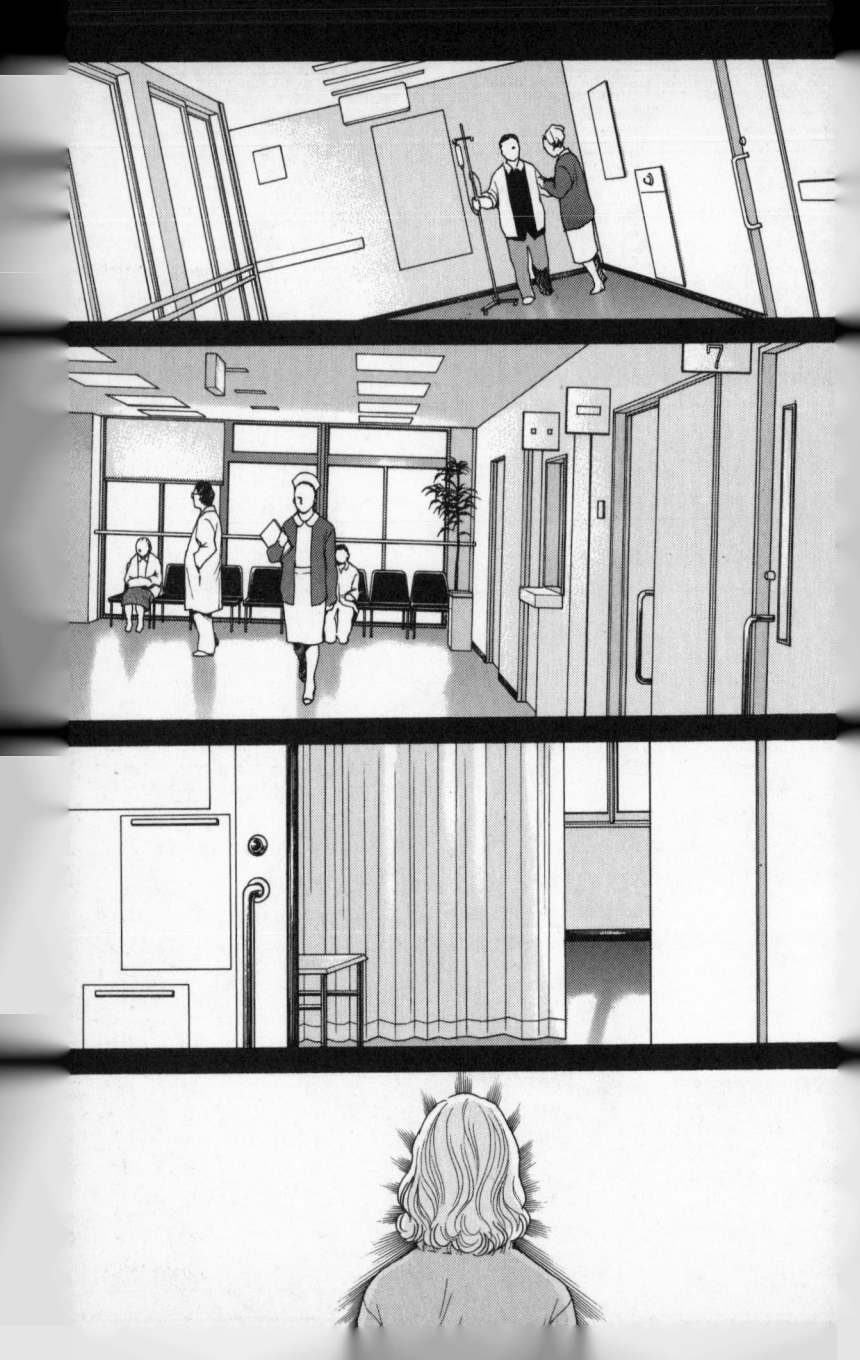

Please repeat what you said...
...doctor.
I mentioned earlier that...
...the injuries to your son's ear and shoulder are not life threatening.
The problem is not his injuries, but the deterioration of his vital organs.

His liver, along with his other vital organs, is beginning to fail.
I don't understand ...?
The easiest way to explain is to tell you that his entire system is aging at an accelerated pace.
Aging? He's only ten years old!
How is this possible?
We're not sure. I do suggest running more tests.
Your son's chronological age is ten years old, but
his body is functioning at the level of a seventy-year-old.
At this rate, I believe he will be confined to a hospital.

Unfor-tunately, we believe...
Confined to a hospital? What's going to happen to my son?
...his condition is terminal.

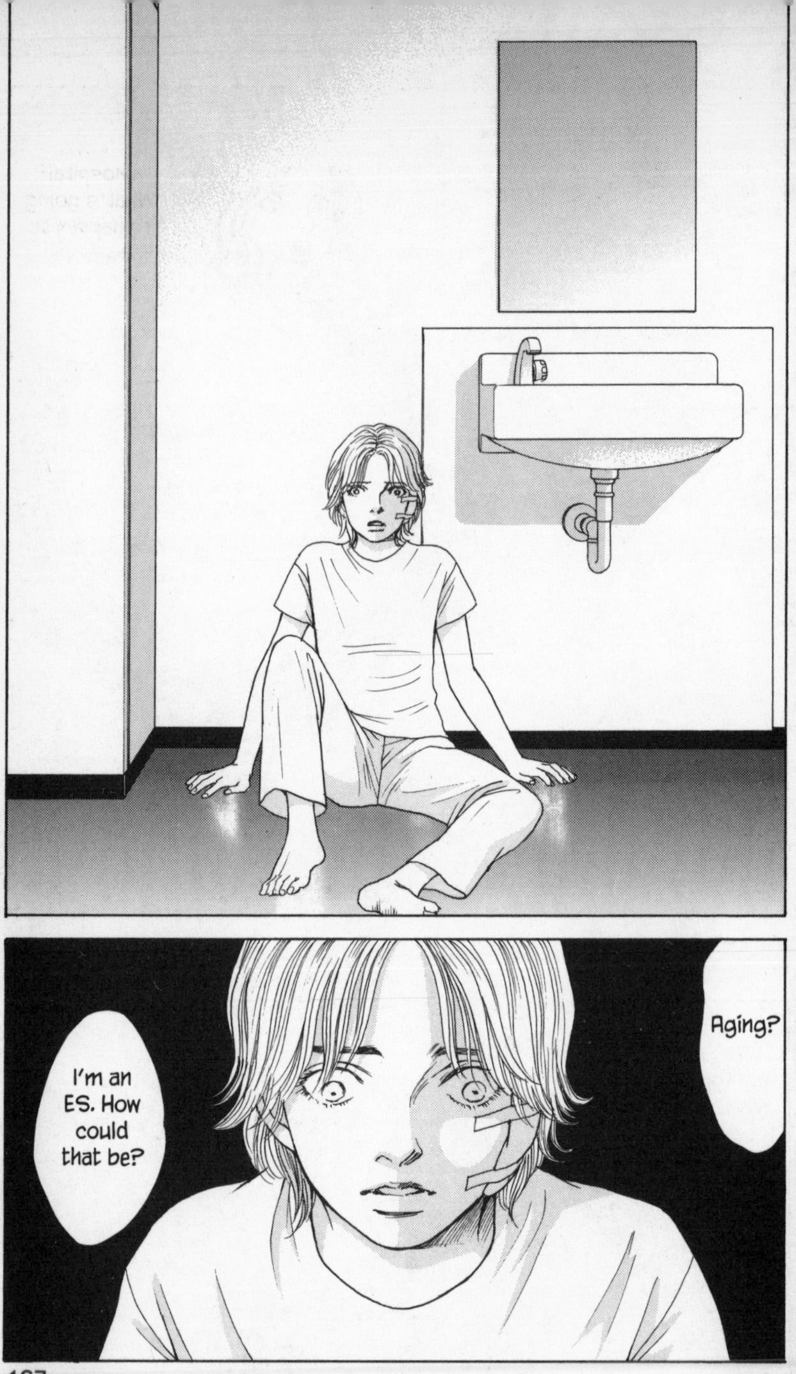
Aging?
I'm an ES. How could that be?

The ES have an advanced immune system.
They are genetically engineered to have an unrivaled biological defense system.
They are the perfect organism.
They can live for over two hundred years...

Two hundred years...?
Those lying bastard scientists!

BASH
Worth-less pieces of crap!
A bunch of brainless idiots!
This is their idea of perfec-tion?
Dammit!
Damn those assholes!

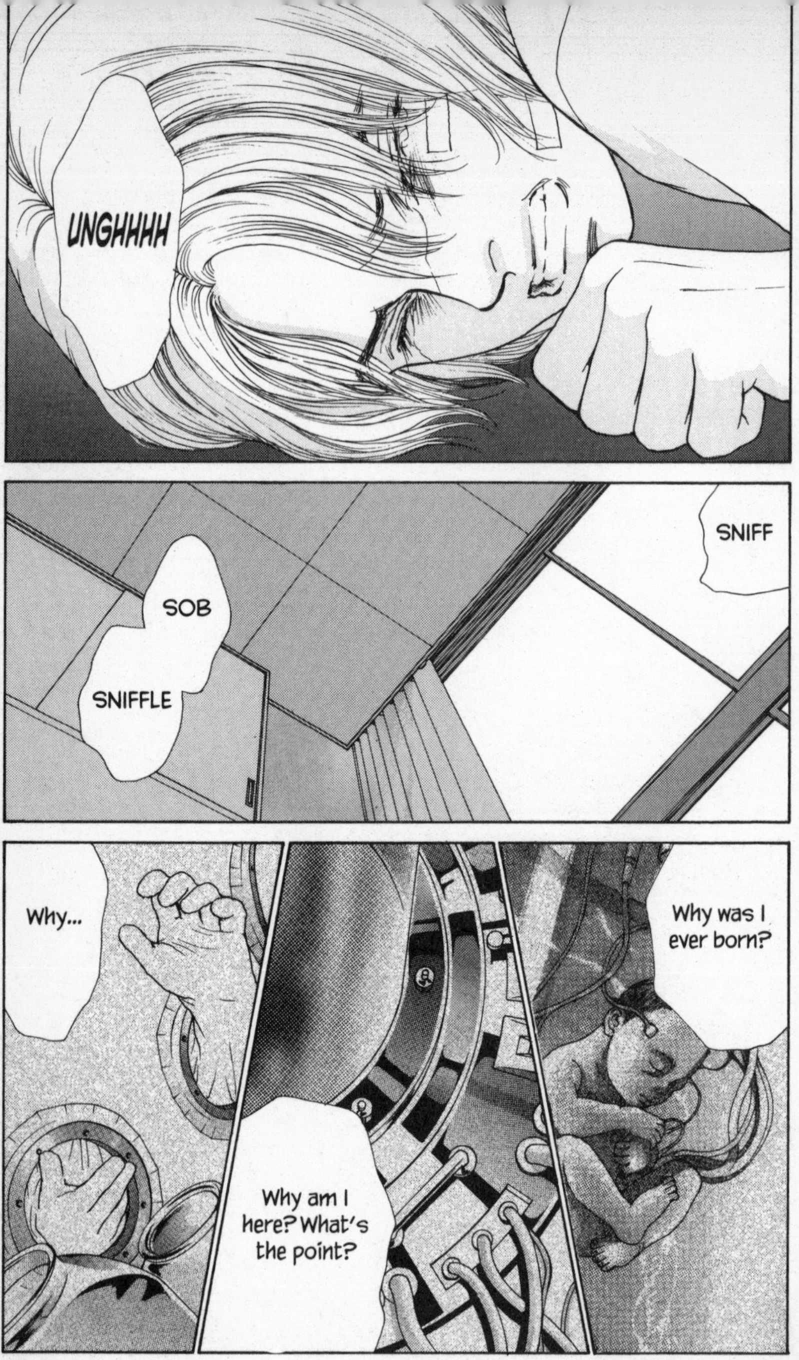
UNGHHHH
SNIFF
SOB
SNIFFLE
Why was I ever born?
Why am I here? What's the point?
Why...

It's over.
I'm going
to die...
...so young...

I'm supposed to be invincible!
I was supposed to have anything I ever wanted...
Heh!
HA
HA
I suppose all things come to an end.
Why do I need such a worth-less world anyway?
I don't need it, so I'm going to destroy it.

I don't need...
...this place...

...anymore.

You're awake.

Where...
Where am I?
The hospital. You were unconscious for a while.
The impact didn't cause damage. Sakaki-san created a quick distraction so we could all get away.
What about Isaac?
What happened to him?

He's still alive.
The gunshot wounds weren't fatal.
I see...
What about the man I shot?
Is he all right?
He's fine. He's injured, but he's in stable condition.
I feel relieved.
PHEW

Were you planning to die?
I was determined to kill Isaac even if it meant I had to die, too.
In the end, I just made an even bigger mess.
I'm sorry.
You had to come to my rescue again.

PA-TAN
He's aging at a rapid pace. He's not going to live for much longer.

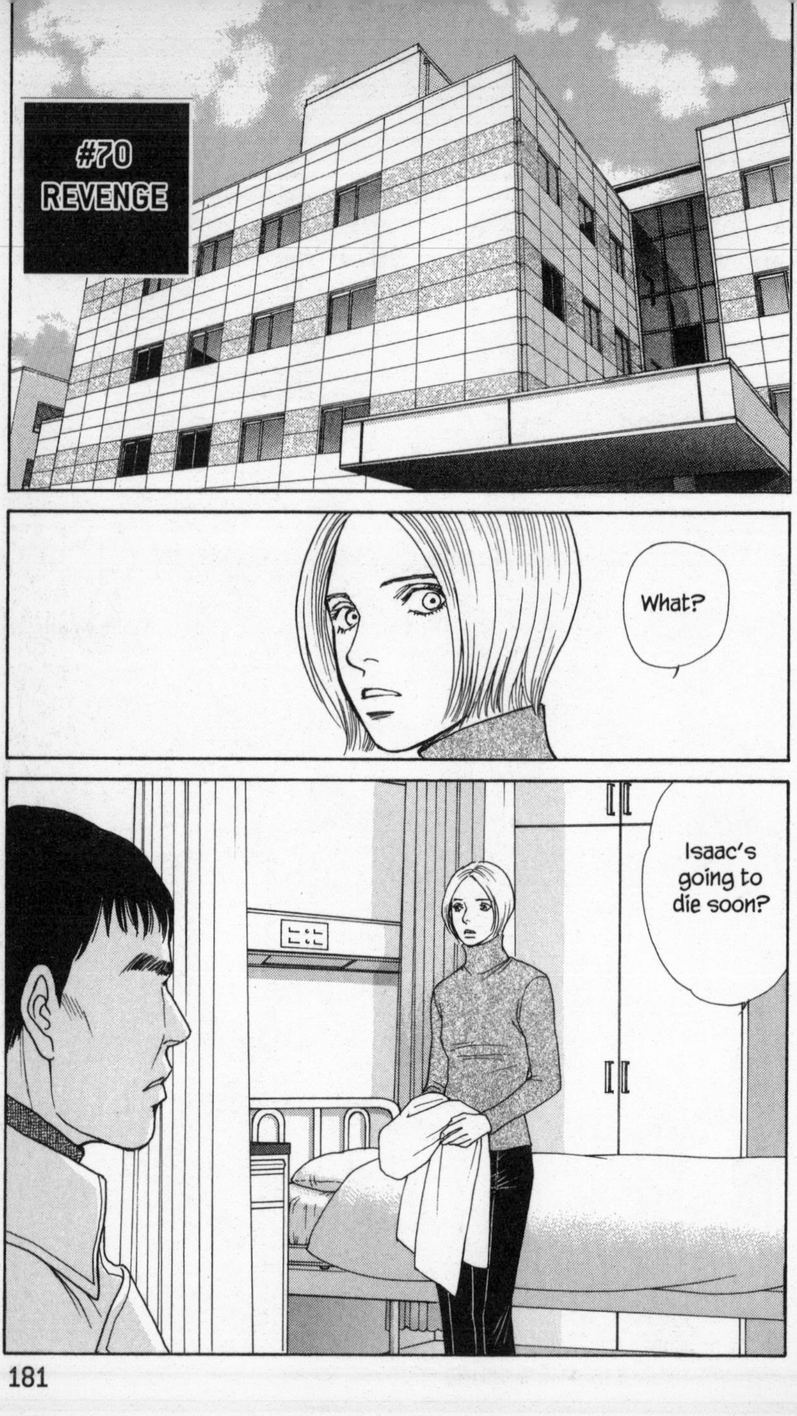
#70
REVENGE
What?
Isaac's going to die soon?

What's going on?
You were right. Isaac has a weakness.
I examined his blood sample and found that he's aging rapidly.
I believe he doesn't have very long to live.
......
I guess Shuro didn't tell you any-thing?
No, he didn't.

I wonder if Isaac is showing any symptoms?
......
I don't know, I haven't looked into that.
I do know...
...that Shuro felt something unusual from Isaac yesterday.

Something unusual? Like what?
When we were trying to get you out of there, we were surrounded by people under Isaac's control. Suddenly, they recovered their senses and let us pass. We barely escaped out of there.
Shuro doesn't believe Isaac let us out alive of his own accord. Something happened to Isaac and he lost control.
An accident?
We don't know, but we can be sure that something bad happened to Isaac.

If I'm right, Isaac will die without any intervention on our part.
We just have to wait for him to weaken and perish.
It's just a matter of patience. He's going to slowly deteriorate.
There's no reason to fear him anymore.
I wonder if Isaac's aware of this.
Huh!?

I wonder if Isaac is aware of his fate?
If he is, do you think he'll be able to accept it?
!
He's used to getting his way, but that's not going to continue for much longer.
Don't you think he'll find a way to take out his anger?
Knowing his personality, I don't think this is going to be an easy ending.

If he decides to focus his anger and despair at the world...
...instead of just us....

MARUGEN 53
MARUGEN 53
!
Check out this kid!
He bleached his hair!
I bet he thinks he's hot shit!

Yo, brat, what are you doing out so late?
グイッ
JERK
Huh?
ボキッ
SNAP
GYAAAAHHHH
FLOP
ブ

GAAAH
Whoa!
Masao, what hap-pened?
ボキッ CRACK
My arm's broken!
My legs!
What happened to my legs!?

!
Hey, kid!
What are you doing out by yourself late at night?
Where's your mom or dad?

BANG
JOLT

Isaac...
SMASH

CRACK
KYAAHHH
CRASH
Somebody call the police!
Where are the cops?
RRRING
RRRING
RRRING

CRACKLE
SMACK
CRACK
SHATTER
WOOOOO
WOOOOO

BOOM
ドォ…ン

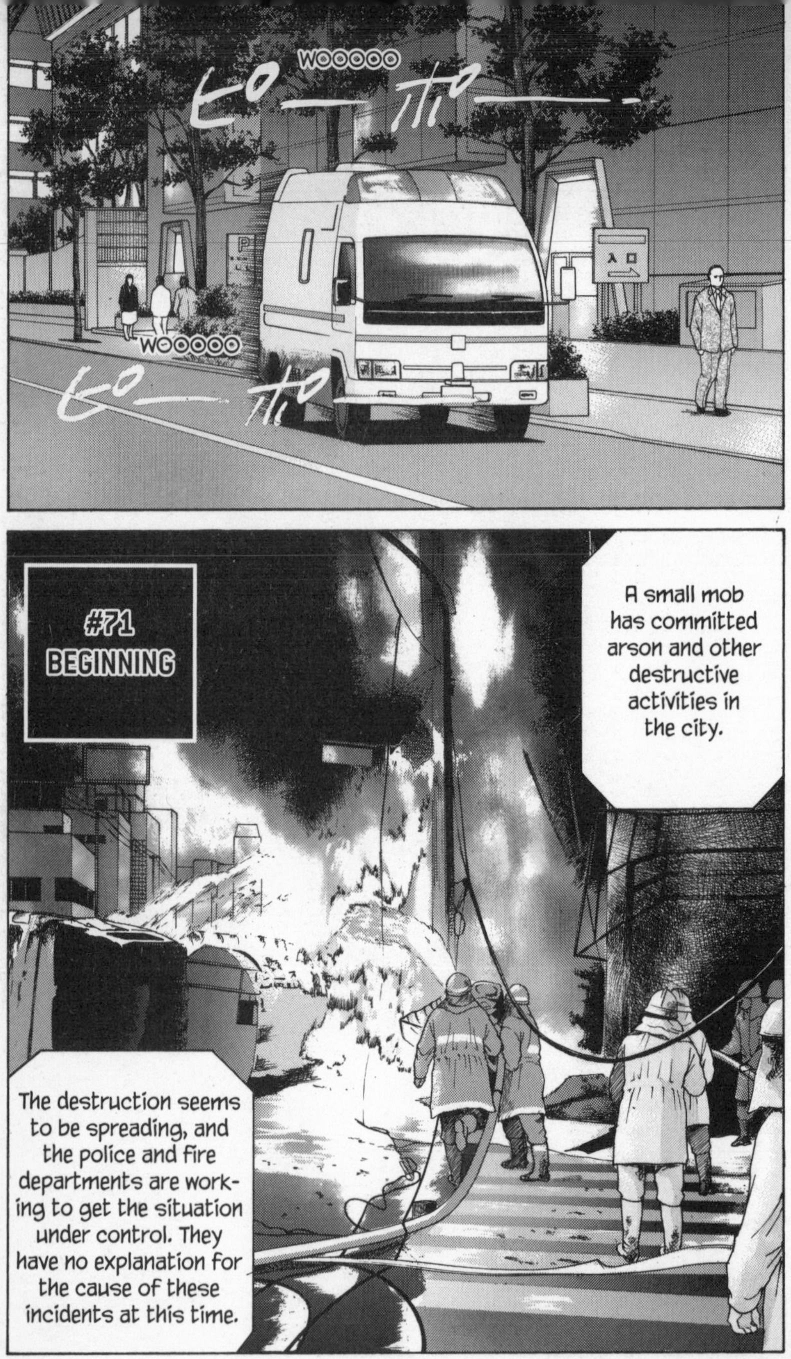
WOOOOO
WOOOOO
#71
BEGINNING
A small mob has committed arson and other destructive activities in the city.
The destruction seems to be spreading, and the police and fire departments are working to get the situation under control. They have no explanation for the cause of these incidents at this time.

Behind me, a car lost control and smashed into a storefront, resulting in multiple injuries.
The fire department has not arrived yet to put out the fire.

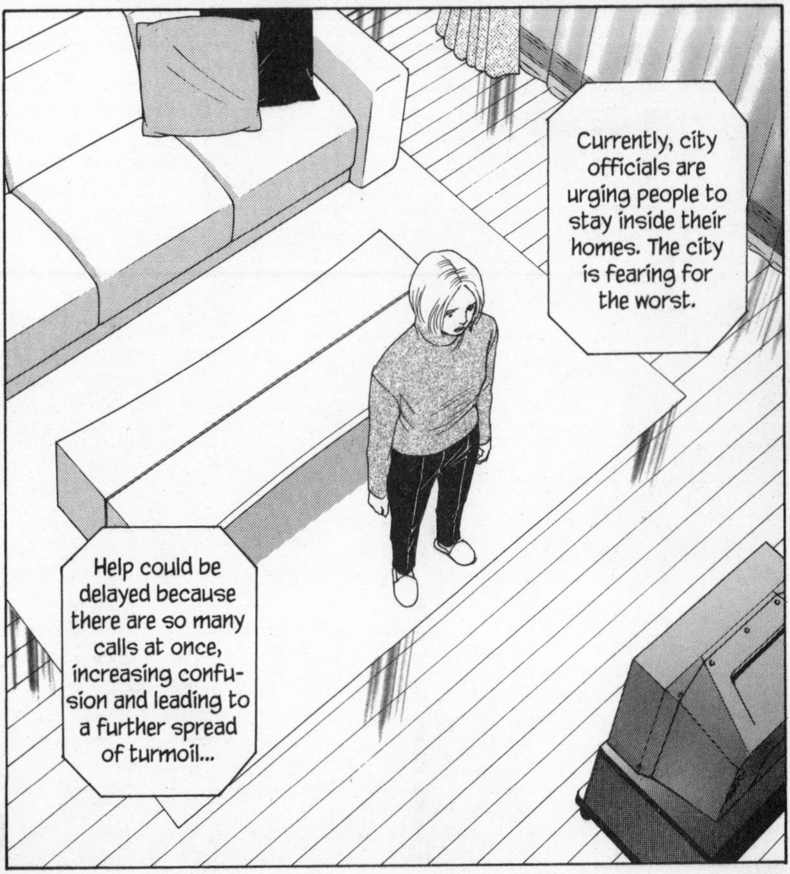
Currently, city officials are urging people to stay inside their homes. The city is fearing for the worst.
Help could be delayed because there are so many calls at once, increasing confu-sion and leading to a further spread of turmoil...

Could this be...
Akiba-kun!?
RRRRING
プルルル…
RRRRING
プルルル
Hello?

Have you been watching TV?
I have. I'm just shocked.
I was just about to call you.
Do you think Isaac's behind this?
I think so.
Did Sakaki-san tell you about Isaac's condition?
Yes, I hear he's aging rapidly...

Do you think his physical condition prompted him to act out like this?
Yes. I don't know his thought process, but I'm sure this is his way of venting his anger.
......
What should we do?
I don't know.
I can't even begin to think...
However...

...I think we're not his only targets anymore.
Either Isaac will die first, or we will.
Or...

...we'll all die together.
That's how things stand.

Oh, well...
I'm sick of this scenery.
I wanna see some-thing more... enter-taining.
I wanna see more violence, more chaos...
The end of the world.

Why didn't I pull the trigger?
I think I missed Isaac on purpose.
I was aiming at his head.
I should have killed him, but I flinched at the very last minute.

Do you know why?
I have no idea.
I was filled with hate and anger until I saw him...
I realize that I sub-consciously missed him on purpose.
I don't think I have the ability to kill.
Mine-san...
It doesn't matter if I'm trying to be cold-blooded or helpful.
I seem to make the situation worse every time...

I think we're partially at fault.
Like Isaac said, we don't have any regard for life.
I think this may be a proper end for that
arrogant and greedy species called human beings...

WOOOOO
ピー ポー
WOOOOO
ピー ポー

City officials are currently...
The damage continues to spread. The police and fire departments have been unable to keep up. The chaos and violence is expected to intensify in this area.
Sakaki-san!
RRRING
RRRING

Are you watching the news?
Yes. It's a mess out there.
The news has been reporting the same story over and over. They haven't been able to resolve any-thing...
So, Isaac is behind all this?
Akiba-kun said he was sure of it.
I think Isaac somehow figured out that he was dying.
This is his way of saying good-bye.
Hah!
His last stand, eh?

I hope this is the end.
I've got a feeling there's more to come.
He wants to take other people out along the way.
I suppose he's the type.
Game over.
We lost.

That's not to say that Isaac won, but
we definitely lost this one.
This game isn't over yet.
In fact, this is the beginning of the real battle.
Sakaki-san?

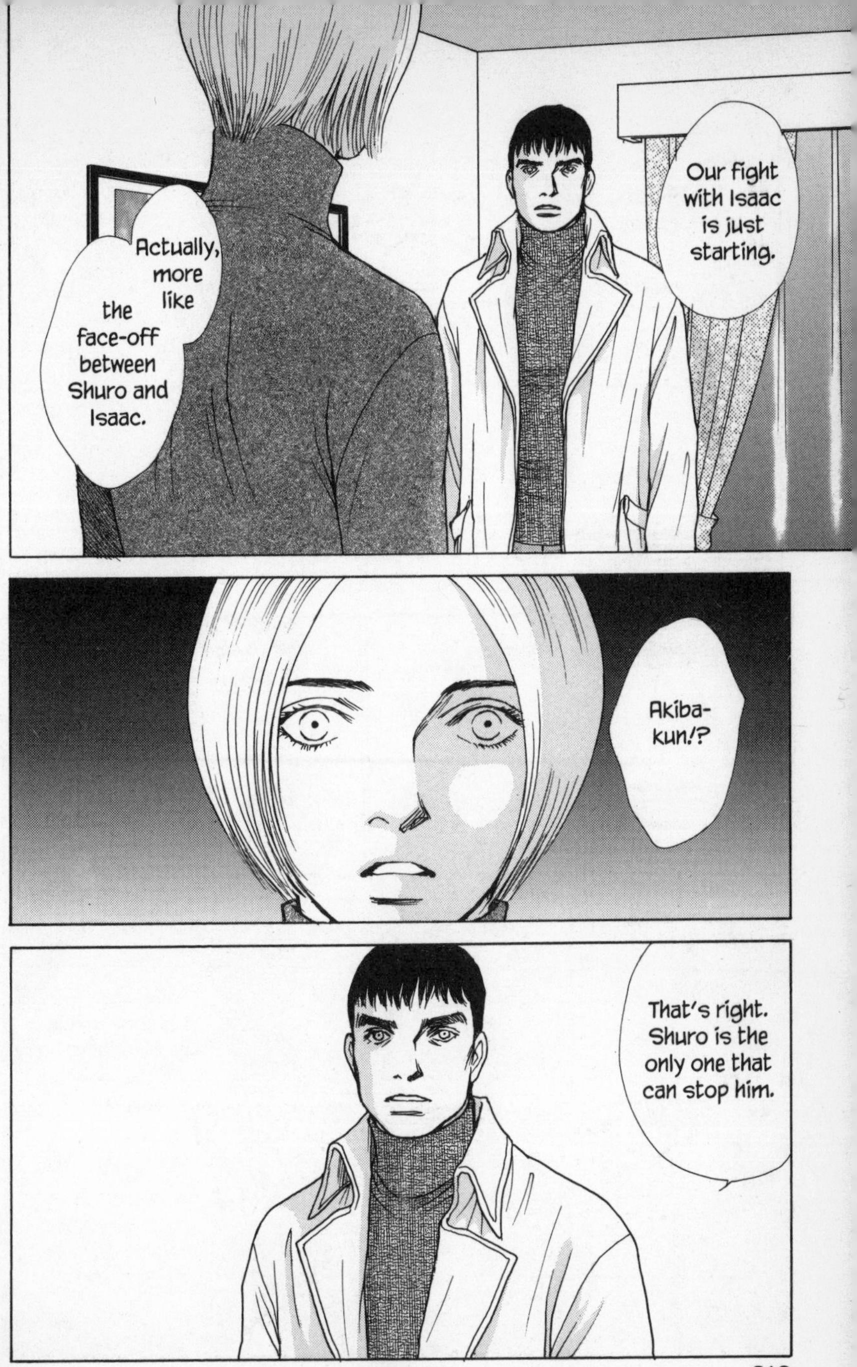
Our fight with Isaac is just starting.
Actually, more like the face-off between Shuro and Isaac.
Akiba-kun!?
That's right. Shuro is the only one that can stop him.

That's impos-sible.
He can't kill Isaac.
Think about it. Isaac is the only family he's got in this world.
In the eyes of the ES, we're the ones that started this whole problem.
Now, they have to kill each other for our sake?
I think it's cruel to ask Shuro to deal with our mistake.
We have no choice. I doubt that Shuro would fight for humanity.
I do know...

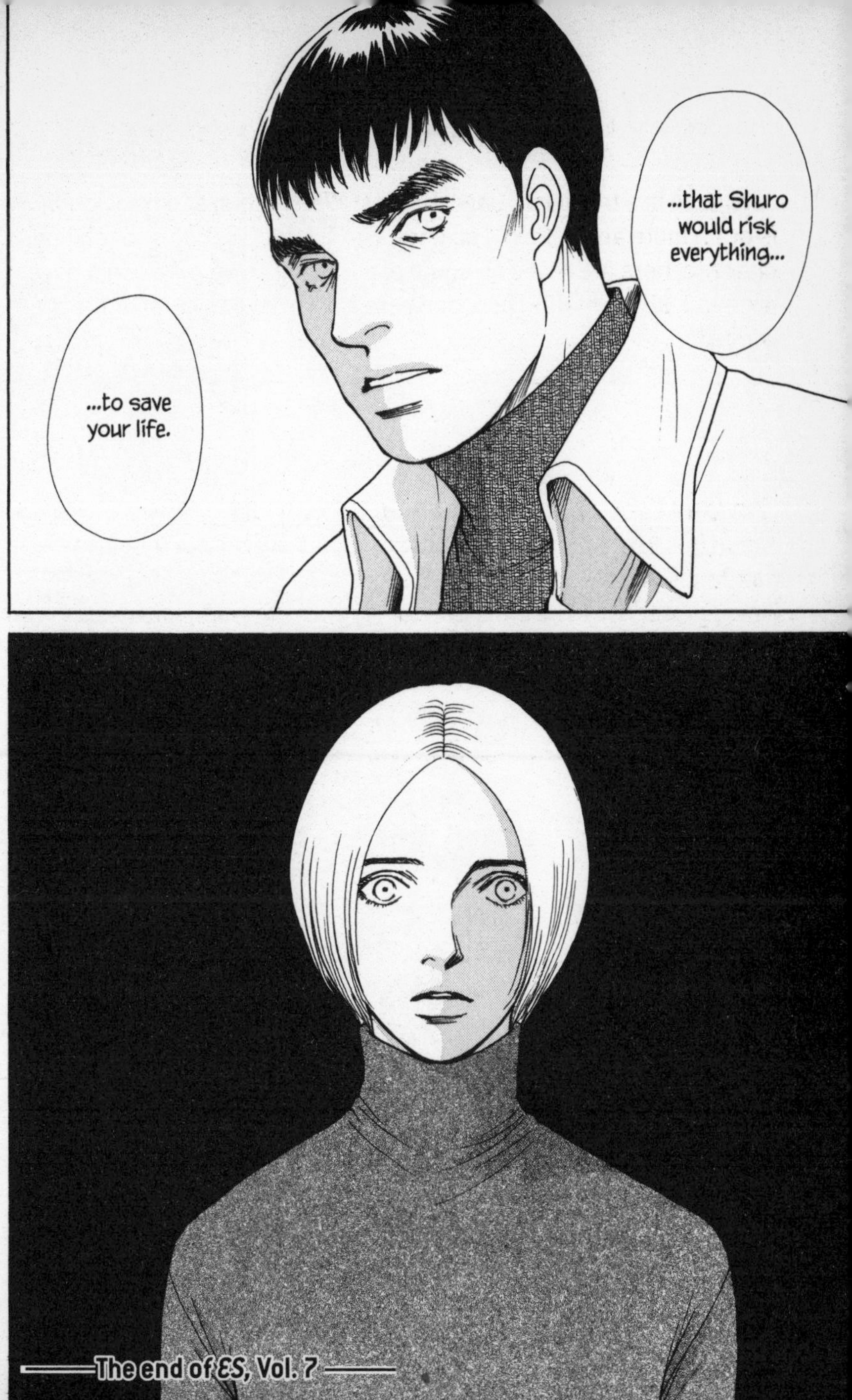
...that Shuro would risk everything...
...to save your life.
The end of ES, Vol. 7

Translation Notes

Japanese is a tricky language for most Westerners, and translation is often more an art than a science. For your edification and reading pleasure, here are notes on some of the places where we could have gone in a different direction, or where a Japanese cultural reference is used.

"I'm glad I learned to shoot a gun...," page 89

Japan has very strict gun-control laws, and civilians cannot own handguns. As a result, shooting ranges are extremely rare in Japan. It's only because Mine once lived in the United States that she knows how to shoot. She would not have the opportunity to learn to shoot in Japan unless she joined the military or pursued a career in law enforcement.

Driving on the left side of the street, page 138

Unlike Americans, the Japanese drive on the left side of the street. Countries that have left-hand driving use vehicles in which the driver's seat is on the right side, as seen below. Roughly 34 percent of the world's driving population drives on the left.

Accelerated aging, page 161

Though Isaac's aging has been accelerated because he's the subject of a genetic experiment, many genetic disorders actually exist that cause symptoms of accelerated aging and abbreviated life spans in humans. Progeria, or Hutchinson-Gilford Progeria syndrome, is one of the more serious and rare types of accelerated-aging disorders.

***Koban*, page 194**

The Japanese police force has a central station along with satellite offices (*koban*) located in each community. The police in each *koban* patrol the area, respond to emergencies, and interact with the community. Below, the police officer is standing outside of the *koban* and keeping watch. In Japan, it is important for the police to have a positive relationship with the community, and it is not unusual for people to approach police officers and start friendly conversations.

Preview of *ƐS*, Vol. 8

We're pleased to present you with a preview of volume 8. Please check our website (www.delreymanga.com) to see when this volume will be available.

本当の高みの見物はおまえかよ。

これから二百年は生きるであろうおまえから見れば
明日死ぬかもしれないオレなんてさぞかし滑稽な存在なんだろうな
思えば同じ遺伝子を持っていながら
スタートラインから違っていたよなおまえとオレって
おまえは生まれながらにエリート
オレは捨て駒——

ドオ゛ン
でも
この世の中では
オレみたいな奴が
たくさんいるらしい
どうあがいても
浮かばれずに
自暴自棄に
なってる奴がね

オレは
そういう連中を
解放してやったのさ
オレを
止めたかったら
ここまで来るん
だな

ALIVE

STORY BY TADASHI KAWASHIMA
ART BY TOKA ADACHI

SMART SCIENCE-FICTION SUSPENSE

Millions of people worldwide have taken their own lives, victims of a lethal alien pandemic visited upon the Earth.

But a group of Tokyo teens has somehow survived and now, facing a devastated world, must ask questions they never thought they'd have to ask:

Why did they abandon us?
Will we be next?
Why are we alive?

Special extras in each volume! Read them all!

VISIT WWW.DELREYMANGA.COM TO:

- Read sample pages
- View release date calendars for upcoming volumes
- Sign up for Del Rey's free manga e-newsletter
- Find out the latest about new Del Rey Manga series

RATING OT AGES 16+

DEL REY MANGA デルレイ
The Otaku's Choice™

Le Chevalier d'Eon

STORY BY TOU UBUKATA
MANGA BY KIRIKO YUMEJI

DARKNESS FALLS ON PARIS

A mysterious cult is sacrificing beautiful young women to a demonic force that threatens the entire country. Only one man can save Paris from chaos and terror, the king's top secret agent: The Chevalier d'Eon.

- Available on DVD from ADV Films.

Special extras in each volume! Read them all!

VISIT WWW.DELREYMANGA.COM TO:

- Read sample pages
- View release date calendars for upcoming volumes
- Sign up for Del Rey's free manga e-newsletter
- Find out the latest about new Del Rey Manga series

RATING OT AGES 16+

DEL REY MANGA デルレイ
The Otaku's Choice™

TOMARE!
[STOP!]

You are going the wrong way!

Manga is a completely different type of reading experience.

To start at the beginning, go to the end!

That's right! Authentic manga is read the traditional Japanese way—from right to left, exactly the opposite of how American books are read. It's easy to follow: Just go to the other end of the book, and read each page—and each panel—from right side to left side, starting at the top right. Now you're experiencing manga as it was meant to be.